They Call Me . . . Pastor Sandy

Girls, I've been around for 31 years and am still going strong! Let me share some of my experiences as a Pastor's Wife; it may bring you healing, restoration and a renewed love for the people and your call.

By Dr. Sandy Toyne
(Dr. of Nouthetic Counseling)

They Call Me . . . Pastor Sandy
Girls, I've been around for 31 years and am still going strong!
Let me share some of my experiences as a Pastor's Wife;
it may bring you healing, restoration and a renewed love
for the people and your call.
by Dr. Sandy Toyne

Printed in the United States of America

ISBN 978-1-60791-739-7

www.xulonpress.com

Table of Contents

Acknowledgments

I want to thank the Lord Jesus Christ for giving me the ability to write this book. It has taken much sacrifice and prayer to complete this assignment, and I could not have done it without Him.

I also want to thank my family for their steadfast support. They always understood the times I was studying or working nonstop to complete an assignment. I'd like to thank Pastor Dennis Toyne, my husband of 38 wonderful years, and my children: my son Steven Toyne with his wife Wendy and two children, Gabi and Rilee; and my daughter Joy Pouwels with her husband Don and their three children, Zachary, Alexis and Michaela. My children have been in ministry with us for over 15 years, and we love them so much.

I would like to thank my mom and brothers and sisters, for supporting me during this time. They encouraged me in my quest for my Doctorate in Nouthetic Counseling, and in the writing of this book, they always offered their proof reading services and gave me honest criticism.

I had a few women in our church that helped me with the first editing of my book: Marlene, Amy, Renee, Bonnie, Karen, I give you all my thanks. And to Sarah Cruz, who put my book all together for me. After home schooling her children all day, she would stay up at night to kindly and ever so gently develop the manuscript and make it into a book, never wanting to take away from my character, but to enhance what I had to say.

FOREWARD

As the husband of Pastor Sandy and also co-pastor with her for over 31 years of ministry, it has been my pleasure to read her book with great admiration of the woman God has given me. As I read this book, it reminds me again and again how God captures every person's heart in such different ways and uses such unusual people in His kingdom. You will laugh out loud as you read the chapter, 'He Captured My Heart'.

Not only is this book a life story, but it is a revelation of how painful ministry can be. You will cry with Pastor Sandy as she unfolds the most horrible times of her life: times of cruel rejection, times of bitter and cutting actions of people whom she trusted, the sorrow of poverty, and the pains of watching her children experience hurts and wounds that others may never face. But, you will also see how we were healed by the love of Father God. This book is real information, a manual, for healing the heart of every pastor. This book is a must read, for anyone in the ministry. Pastor Sandy's stories remind us of how God is such a wonderful Father to pastors and is willing to help us in the most troubling of times.

As you are reading the accounts or Pastor Sandy's life, you will have memories of your own to come to the surface. At this time, it is very important for you to pray the prayers at the end of the chapter: prayers of healing, forgiving people, and cleansing of the soul. As you do, you will sense the loving healing arms of Father God wrap around you bringing peace, healing and comfort to you. You will have a great time with this book. I trust you will enjoy it as much as I have.

Pastor Dennis Toyne

Chapter 1

He Captured My Heart

I was raised by my dear mom and dad in a close knit family of eleven. Of the nine children birthed, I was the eldest of three daughters, having two older brothers and four younger brothers. For the first part of my life I was raised with just the boys. My younger sisters and baby brother were like a second family, since the youngest was born seventeen years after my eldest brother. With little spacing between each birth, we were the prime example of what was termed a "stair step" family. Although we were poor, we didn't even realize it. The combination of our closeness in age, and being raised at the same time made us an extremely close knit family. You could say we were a rag tag bunch of kids in a growing neighborhood of other rag tag kids! It was actually quite enjoyable growing up where and when we did in the 1950's and 60's.

My father had been a WWII drill sergeant in the US Army; before settling down into family life with his little bunch of rascals. Like many others coming from that post-war era, we just wanted to start life afresh. Many returned home from the war as heroes with new zeal, determined to make up for lost time. The eager spirit of America was clear: we had won the war and were now ready to get on with our lives.

Yet things didn't unfold quite the way many of these hard-fighting men and women envisioned in those fox holes of Germany and France. For Dad, his return from war was a sad and difficult time for he drank excessively. At times he relived the war by way of his dreams, and suddenly he would awake crying or yelling. While napping on the couch he'd be awakened by this type of dreams. Disoriented, he actually thought we were the enemy! Poor dad. He never hurt us, but he found himself embarrassed when he regained his senses and realized he had done such a thing.

I can still hear Mom assuring him, "You're all right. You're in your home." When I grew older, and he continued to have such dreams, I would repeat those same reassuring words I heard Mom express. Even as children we were conscious not to make much of a fuss so Dad wouldn't have to explain himself to a group of kids sitting around viewing their favorite TV program.

Dad drank heavily the first 24 years of my life. During those years we never knew when Dad would be coming home, or in what condition we would find him. Finally, around age 52, he quit.

Living in a War Zone

There is one specific incident is etched within the recesses of my mind and emotions. Dad had arrived home very late and began feuding with Mom. I was awakened by horrific screams and shouted threats. Mom hollered, "Get out and never come back!" Objects flew across the room, hitting the wall while Dad yelled for Mom to stop. Mom would then pinch Dad, while he slapped her hand. This sort of thing played out for a time.

As the oldest daughter I felt compelled to get them to stop. I timidly crept downstairs and stood by the kitchen door. I fearfully watched their looks of hatred towards each other. When they finally noticed me, those angry looks suddenly became focused upon me! But before I could blurt out the words, "Please, stop fighting!" Dad angrily demanded, "Sandra Marlene, you shut your mouth and get back up to bed!"

The help I thought I could offer only ended in their turning spite toward me. And, I didn't even know what their fight was about! Only God knew what had been going on in the midst of their never-ending feud. They never shared this with anyone, which in a sense was honorable. They knew how to fight and they went hard at it!

Those mornings after those fights, before I went downstairs, I would wonder if Dad would be sitting in his usual place, reading his newspaper, drinking his coffee. And he always was. No matter what transpired during the night, Dad would always greet me in the same manner, "Good Morning Sandy Marlene." Never as much as looking up from the paper, this was said without a smile. Yet in a sense, this greeting gave me a great sense of security.

Mom, she'd be cooking breakfast, trying to get all of us up and ready for school. Life did not necessarily change much — no one died in the night and no one left us. It was as if there was this unspoken understanding that we had to be prepared for whatever came our way. We could be the victims and this made us tough as nails, ready for anything.

From the perspective of us nine children trying to sleep through those fights, those were nights from hell. I remember vividly, my little girl frame, standing often at the top of those steps crying and begging for the fighting to stop. It seemed our feelings did not matter at this particular stage of their life. I vowed at a very young age that I would not allow anyone to control me or treat me like they did one another. I realized as well that I would never give into the generational curse of alcoholism. I had a longing to rise above that which I'd been exposed to; that which had instilled many insecurities and fears in my life. My parents did not understand the impact their combative feuds had on us. We all felt compelled to choose sides, either Mom or Dad, often based upon words we heard come forth from their mouths. We judged and sided up, most of the time I took Dad's side, like most little girls do toward their daddy's. I felt Mom was unfair to Dad. I was just happy when he came home. I did not understand Mom's feelings of betrayal and rejection when Dad stayed out until the bars closed in the wee hours of the night. I was a young girl in a cocoon of innocence. I was a little girl who just wanted her Daddy home, yet all I heard was Mom commanding, "Get out and never come back!" If Dad was drunk on whiskey, Mom was drunk on anger and resentment. Their behaviors were an endless cycle. As a child, you do not understand theses marital dynamics. Mom was really the one that held the marriage together by a thread all those years.

Dad was not a binge drinker. He just never ceased drinking. Whiskey chased down by a beer began his day. Bottles of hard liquor were hidden outside. Each night he would return with a new six-pack in a brown paper sack under his arm. Before the night was over, the beer was gone. This caused many problems as the boys got older and needed discipline. He was under the influence of alcohol many times, and he did not know how to correct them without harsh words and actions. This caused a constant friction in the family. It seemed there was no rest or peace — just constant fighting, yelling and contempt in our home.

In All This Mess. . . .

In the midst of all this mess, my mom came to Christ and was saved during an Oral Roberts Tent Revival in Minneapolis in the early 1960's. This was the beginning of change in our lives as a family as we knew it. Mom seemed to fall into a legalistic holiness doctrine, carrying the thinking that everything under the sun was a sin. Activities which had been considered normal for us were now no longer permitted. Attending a movie theater, bowling, skating, and going to the circus, fairs, and all the normal, fun things we knew as children, were now considered sin! We were even told it would send us to hell! Well, I certainly didn't want to end up in hell, so I never went to another 'worldly' event with the help of my Mom's strict supervision.

We tried desperately to make sense of why what was had once been so fun, now was deemed so sinful. Although confused I did my best to understand. My older brothers became increasingly bitter. Prior to this time, we had been attending a great church with a youth group that the boys actually enjoyed. Yet mom wanted to switch churches because she did not believe the grace message the minister had been preaching. Thus began the downfall of my brothers. Our new preacher, a woman, believed and promoted the 'everything was sin doctrine.' Under her leadership, parents were directed to not allow their children to participate in worldly activities. In time my brothers became rebellious because every fun activity was stripped away. They finally decided if they were going to go to hell, they'd go having fun!

I recall one Easter Sunday in particular. Mom dressed us up fine and sent us off to church. I do not recall if my parents had been there this time or not since dad had a tendency to drop us off at the front door. He would give each of us a quarter for the offering, and return when the church service was over to take us home. As dad drove away my brothers and I would head down to the local mom and pop shop and buy candy before church instead of putting it into the offering! When we finally did enter the church that particular Easter Sunday, I walked down the aisle and sat myself in the very front row with my fancy little dress, my new Easter hat and white shoes. It amazes me today that after 53 years, I still like to dress my very best for church and marched up the aisle and sit in the front row just like I did many years ago at the Calvary Baptist Church.

Mom was ever-faithful to keep each of us in the House of God. We attended our Pentecostal church three times a week; it was back in the days when preachers did not take into consideration how long a service or message lasted. They just preached and sang until they were finished, whether God showed up or not. Despite all that I actually loved the church. The pastors were super nice folks, and I found myself wanting to be to be like them.

He Captured My Heart

As I reflect back upon those painful early years, I believe God was preparing me to minister the gospel of Jesus Christ. It was at this young age the Lord began to capture my heart! How does anyone know what their life will be like, especially when a child? Yet it seemed as though from a young girl on I had a propensity toward spiritual things.

The first time I said the Prayer of Salvation, Mom was at the altar in a Pentecostal church. She always made me go to the altar with her while she prayed (probably to keep an eye on me). I must have been five years old, and I began to whine in mom's ear. I was done, no longer wanting to be up there and whatever she was saying to God I didn't care. My knees were even falling asleep! When the preacher came by to check on Mom, he thought I was praying and crying out to God. I was simply tired and complaining, yet he mistook the situation and used it as an opportunity for me, this lost sinner, to get saved. Consequently, at the age of five, I said my first sinner's prayer; something I've done every Sunday since. When my dear husband, Pastor Dennis, gives an altar call, I love praying along with those giving their lives to the Lord Jesus Christ. Some things never change.

My next encounter with the Lord was at the age of twelve, when a Pentecostal tent revival came into town. What great times these were! The week-long event was held in a tent on my Aunt Dena's property. We filled that tent with an old piano my Dad bought and old wooden chairs. A make shift pulpit was placed in the midst straw bales that served as an altar of prayer.

The Revivalist had a wife who played and sang along with their three handsome young sons. Those three boys were so very nice, especially the oldest boy. Now remember, I was raised with six brothers of my own and a drill sergeant for a dad so there was not much affection in our home. We had no use or no time taken for the kissing and hugging I witnessed within the Revivalist's family. My family was more apt to give you a good poke as a token of their affection!

So one day, these kissing, affectionate boys, wanted to play a game after the service and you guessed it, it was a game that involved kissing! We kids were left unattended to run around and play in the night while the adults prayed in the tent. Now, this particular game entailed that of tag, and if you were "tagged," you got kissed. Sure enough, one of those bold, affectionate boys caught me on my Aunt Dena's front porch, as I hung on to that front door for dear life. He may have hoped for a kiss, but instead he got a good hard poke! He wasn't very happy, and neither was I. I had no clue how to kiss a boy.

I found myself embarrassed and mad. I headed back to the tent where I knelt down by a bail of hay. I was disappointed at my behavior; not so much for doing anything wrong, but because I didn't know how to kiss a boy! I headed to the tent and knelt by a bale of straw. As I did, the presence of the Holy Spirit captured my heart. There I was, a foolish, self-centered little girl, but God captured me regardless of my frailties. I sensed something I hadn't sensed before – a very tangible presence of God's great love. Forget those boys! I now felt the very presence of God Himself. Captured in the moment, I cried out like a baby and asked God to make me a minister of the Gospel. I was no longer the little five year old girl at the altar. Now at the age of accountability, I understood beyond the shadow of a doubt my desire to serve Jesus the rest of my life! My heart was truly changed.

What's The Big Deal?

My next spiritual marker came when I was fourteen years old. I had new friend who came from a large family and invited the children to church; crying and praying out to God with the pastors this bunch of kids were saved. I was amazed by how they each instantly responded to the prayer of salvation. As I watched, I thought, "what's the big deal?" Suddenly, I felt God's unmistakable presence, and it was like God again was sealing the Call on my life by revealing how important it was for me to bring people not only to church but to bring and introduce them to the living God! I knew then and there, there's no turning back! My heart may have been moving toward God in the awkward stages of life, and even through some very trying times in our family of eleven, but it was a done deal as far as I was concerned.

As my brothers and I grew older in our family's dysfunction, the boys walked away from the church. Dad took over the disciplinarian role with the boys while Mom would discipline the girls and baby brother. Picture light and dark within our family: the light was Mom embracing the legalistic doctrine, and the dark was Dad, a lawless alcoholic. Dad did what he thought was right in his own eyes, allowed the boys to do the same, until they eventually landed in trouble with the law. Then, Dad would punish them for being so stupid. I, on the other hand, was pulled into Mom's world of excessive rules dictated by a great fear of going to hell. Looking back, I now believe Mom's holiness was a safe place, filled with ready-made rules, since she lived with a man who had no rules.

Eventually the eldest three brothers went off to Viet Nam. All three came back alive, thank God, but two had suffered tremendously. Seeing what happened to her sons, Mom did all she could to shelter me from the world. She understood the call of God on my life, yet she felt she should come alongside God and help Him out a bit!

Mom made it difficult when it came to dating. I was not allowed to date young men outside of our Pentecostal religion. Additionally, my big brother took it upon himself to instruct the neighborhood boys that his sister was "off limits." Yet I had no idea he did that. My nick name among my brothers was "Ugly," and often I wondered if they even knew my real name. As a result of all this, I had a complex. It was not until years later when my brother Mark confessed to me what he did; he used this as a method of watching out for his baby sister. That explained a lot!

Only the Preacher Boys

As a result of Mom's dating policy for me, I always looked forward to each Revival to see if the Evangelist brought any young preachers. We called them "glorified tent boys." These boys would put up the tents and sleep on the grounds around the tent to protect it from vandalism and storms. Most of them knew how to play piano or guitar so they could help lead worship.

I can count on one hand how many I got to know over the years as they all seemed to have a girlfriend in each town. Those boys were just waiting for the right one to come along so they could marry her, and they were super picky. The girl had to be pretty, but most of all, the girl had to know how to play the piano and sing. It seemed they weren't marrying for love; they were marrying for a ministry partner. It's amazing how desperate some of them were! Nearly every girl had a story about those young preachers asking for their hand in marriage.

I met my true love by what appeared to be a fluke, but I believe it was truly the hand of God. At the time I was "supposedly" engaged to a preacher's kid, but we did not see much of each other. It was a rather strange relationship, as this young man was rebellious and backslidden. His father and mother wanted him to marry me so that he could straighten out. He was not willing to settle down and was very deceitful toward me. Finally, he let me go, and it was the best thing that could have happened to me for many reasons.

Crazy things can materialize in a church when a person pronounces they have heard from God, when in reality they have not. A 56-year old man thought God spoke to him that he ought to marry me. I was only sixteen years old at the time, and he quietly waited in the background for me to come to my senses and marry him instead! This man actually went to my pastors and revealed his bank account. Evidently he had a supply of cash, so he said to the pastors, “If you agree that I marry Sandy, I will buy you a new Cadillac.” Well, thankfully that went over like a lead balloon! This man then had the audacity to head to my parent’s house and ask my Mom the same thing! As I watched from the window Mom’s hands stationed on her hips in what looked like shock and horror. Boy, did that short, little woman of four feet, eleven inches give that man a tongue lashing! I believe if Dad would have been around that day, Mr. Money Bags would not have made it home! Yet for some odd reason our church did not kick him out.

I entered my twenties with a broken heart. I was mad at God for my failed engagement, and I was mad about the old guy dogging my trail. Lonely, confused and somewhat immature, I decided I would try to win back my lost fiancée. To do so, the first step in the matter was a decision I made to backslide.

At the time, I was renting a room at the YWCA for $9 per week. I literally lived on popcorn, 7-Up and freedom! I was proud to live on my own, and I loved meeting all the college girls who, like me, were on their own for the first time. Since I was determined to win my guy back, I asked one of the girls who owned a car to drive me 90 miles away, to his hometown. Without hesitation, she agreed!

Thankfully, the Lord had bigger plans than mine. On this cold snowy night in February, the frigid Iowa weather was -30 degrees, not including wind chills! 28 miles from home, the rods blew in my friend’s vehicle. We walked to a little farm community, and thankfully a store was open. I did not want to call anyone to come and get us, so my friend volunteered to call some college friends.

Two very handsome boys picked us up, asking if we wanted to go back to the dorms with them. My friend agreed and looked at me to say, “Sandy, you do not want to go to the dorms.” I looked her squarely and intently in the face with a determined will to backslide and said "Yes I do!" I was still working on my plan.

A short while later I found myself sitting on a bed in a small dorm room with five people. Someone brought out a liquor bottle and handed me a drink. I will never forget the words I spoke to them as long as I live, "Sorry guys, I am in the wrong place! I am saved, filled with the Holy Ghost and called to preach the Gospel of Jesus Christ, and I do not drink." They were dumbfounded; all they managed to say "You need to meet the guy who sleeps in the bed you're sitting on." I left the dorm feeling curious about this fellow.

Although I attempted to turn my back on the Lord, He did not turn his back on me. I left there feeling as though this Call placed so powerfully on my life was much stronger than me. It only took until the next evening for the realization of this to have a great impact upon me. Like a good girl, I went to church. It was during an evening service where we had a Holy Ghost blow out (Pentecostal terminology). At the end of the service while I was busy talking one of my pastors came up to me she pointed her finger at me and spoke these words: "Do not let him get away!"

I knew exactly who this pastor was talking about. He was a young man from the college who often attended Sunday evenings, but I had been so shy that I never spoke with him. Encouraged by my pastor's words, this time would be different. As I approached him I felt as I did so often, not knowing exactly what to say. So, I decided to ask him if he knew the fellow I had met the night before. This young man not only knew him, he was his roommate! My facial expression told him that I was the girl that had sat on the edge of his bed just the night before. Mortified, I swore him to secrecy, since no one else knew what I had attempted that night.

Well, we began by going out on a date that very night, and we've been together ever since for over 37 years! Dennis is the love of my life and my very best friend. The Lord interrupted both our plans in order to divinely place us together. We have been very happy in the ministry all these years and raising two beautiful and talented children, both of whom work alongside us in the ministry.

Dear Ol' Dad

I would be remiss if I did not disclose the end of my Dad's story. At the age of seventeen, I preached my first sermon. Was I nervous! I gave my first altar call, and Dad just happened to come that Sunday morning to listen to me preach. Like most "new preachers," I said everything I knew in about ten minutes. I preached out of John 5:1-9 with the title, "Will You Be Made Whole?" I had no idea what to say with the exception of the title of the sermon! The rest was left up to God. When I gave that first altar call, Dad came up. Was he a sinner in need and want of a Savior? Yes, but I was not certain how serious he was that day. It took Dad a few years before finally deciding to live for Jesus Christ, but what an honor to have planted that seed into his life. Others later watered it, and finally the harvest was brought forth!

Mom began to also sense the call of God on her life. She had been an adult Sunday School teacher for years and she loved the Word of God. When she left the church we'd been raised in, she announced to Dad she wanted to preach. Enough said. Dad was going to make this happen for his wife.

We had a huge garden on the lot beside the home we grew up in. Dad went out and found a nice white house that could be moved. He moved that house onto the land and there he made a place for Mom to preach. He put out a sign and an old bell to ring in the people, as well as a sign. What a wonderful love-offering Dad gave Mom after all those years of dysfunction and pain. Every Sunday Dad sat in the right hand corner of that church. He never preached but was a faithful member of *Fort Dodge Temple of Praise* until he became ill. They then closed the church doors. Mom then cared for her ill husband. They were faithful companions, Mom praying and caring for Dad for five years while he was sick, never regretting the time spent with him. Their last years were devoted to each other in a reaffirming love that began so many years ago. God has a marvelous way of restoring what the locust has eaten.

Chapter 2

The Pastor's Wife

A Class of Our Own

The pastor's wife, queen of the parsonage, if you please, we are a unique class of people. By just our title alone, something is often expected of us that we may not be able to give. This title comes along with our husband's office, and undeniably people will expect certain things from us. People will expect, demand, pull and sometimes push us into their world. Some of us go willingly, out of a caring heart or the mutual call to shepherd the sheep. Others will wonder what they got themselves into by marrying a man who was called to pastor.

Thankfully, Peter wrote of what was expected of the pastor's wife. Having a wife himself, he must have known people would be asking. After all, no one wants to step into the unknown without a little knowledge of what will be required of them.

Several other valuable books have been written about the pastor's wife; however, not much was available when I entered the pastorate thirty-one years ago. Back then, we all went into this adventure with the carefree attitude of "what could be so hard about pastoring a church?"

Which Type are You?

For those raised inside the church, it may be a different story, since we had great role models from the own pastor's wife. How wonderful it would be to follow the footsteps of your beloved pastor's wife and have her right there to mentor you. That would be the ideal way to enter the ministry, but for those who were not raised in the church, this could be very difficult. Whatever the case may be, we have all had many experiences, both good and bad, and that helped form who we are today.

From the way I see it, there are two classes of Pastors' wives. First, we have the wives who feel that their husband's spiritual call is also their call. These women are also pastors and hold both authoritarian and ministerial responsibilities. Second, we have the wives who married a pastor, but decided to leave the ministering to the Pastor. Some of these women sought careers outside the ministry. Some are full time mothers and housewives.

The Qualifications of an Elder, Bishop, Pastor, and Overseer:

In 1 Timothy 3:1-7 and Titus 1:5-9, we see that we do have an obligation. Paul gives Titus detailed instructions on how to set the church in order and the qualifications of what the church is actually searching for when hiring a preacher to pastor a church:

> *For this cause left I thee in Crete, that thou shouldest set in order the things that are wanting, and ordain elders in every city, as I had appointed thee: If any be blameless, the husband of one wife, having faithful children not accused of riot or unruly. For a bishop must be blameless, as the steward of God; not self-willed, not soon angry, not given to wine, no striker, not given to filthy lucre; But a lover of hospitality, a lover of good men, sober, just, holy, temperate; Holding fast the faithful word as he hath been taught, that he may be able by sound doctrine both to exhort and to convince the gainsayers. (Titus 1:5-9 KJV)*

Understanding the Scriptures can set you free from the bondage that people will put on you. First of all, men do not choose you to be part of the five-fold ministry. That is a direct call from the Lord himself. Paul said that he did not confer with flesh and blood. This is where some people make their mistake. These qualifications are valid to the church government, but man does not choose us, we are chosen by God.

Church government is governed by qualifications; the Holy Spirit does the calling. It does not excuse us to live any way we want; we can disqualify ourselves by our lifestyle. These Scriptures are to set up the church government and how to choose quality leaders to govern the church body.

1. **Blameless:** un-accused, i.e. (by implication) irreproachable[1]

Some of these qualifications are very tough to accept since many people feel like they are called to minister the Gospel, yet it is difficult since some have made grave mistakes before they became Christians and their reputation follows them. It may be hard for people to forget the past even though the Lord has. Remember, these rules are given to protect the pastors and church, not to punish anyone for their past life.

If someone who is not an upright man or woman is stationed in a leadership position in the church it can wreak havoc in the church. This is why it is wise to know who you are allowing to come up along side of you to minister to your people. In this day and age, it is easy to do background checks as well as watch a person to see if they are indeed a new creature, through the new birth, remembering that we also stand on the Blood of Jesus Christ to wash all our sins away. (II Cor. 5:17 KJV)

2. The Husband of One Wife

There are many opinions and stances on this piece of Scripture. It has always seemed unfair to me. I am the wife of one husband; we have never been involved in divorce. However, there are many people who have experienced this pain, to their regret. I have tried my best to come to some resolution according to the Scriptures and not rewrite the Bible for my own use. However, while some organizations will completely write off a minister of God's Word or an up-and-coming young man or woman who made this mistake of divorce, I cannot find any part of Scripture to give anyone the right to refuse others the call on their life because they are divorced.

A noted Greek scholar explains that this scripture means one wife at a time. His argument is that if a minister is divorced it would have to be an unpardonable sin, which it is not. There are acceptable reasons for people to get a divorce in New Testament times and it did not say they would be disqualified from ministries if they did so. Desertion and adultery are two good reasons to depart from a marriage.

The divorce rate within the church is the same as that of the world. While this is a very sad statement, I believe there can be extenuating circumstances in each situation. We need to judge each situation individually so that those who are called can actually fulfill the call of God on their life. If, on the other hand, we think that divorce disqualifies someone from ever being part of the leadership of a church, this narrows down the amount of anointed, gifted, and talented people available to do the work of the ministry and edify the body of Christ. This is especially true since 50% of people being divorced are inside the church, which is a shame. What a mockery of the plan of forgiveness, and restoration this would make.

3. Having Faithful Children Not Accused of Riot or Unruly

a. Faithful: Trustworthy; subjectively, trustful: KJV— believe (-ing, -r), faithful (-ly), sure, true [2]

We personally went through a very rough time in the church regarding this qualification. When our children back slid, we were trying to bring them back in under our control. They were coming around when the church judged us as not having our children under control and therefore unfit for the ministry. This was not the time to throw us out. This was the time to support us through prayer. We had already been in a successful ministry for about fifteen years. It was too late for them to decide if we were qualified. It was a done deal; the call of God was in our life, but our kids became rebellious for a season in their teenage years. What a disgrace for our church to throw us away. We lost the battle for a period of time, due to the devil's tactic to divide and conquer. The church failed to pass the test of grace and support of the pastors or anyone going through a trial of life. We moved on, but all the resentment our children had against the people for what they did chased them further away from church. They judged the church as unfair and filled with self-righteous hypocrites. I do thank God that it did not take them long to come fully back to Jesus, and eventually the church. They were never far away from Him, but the church had hurt them badly. At the judgment seat of Christ, who will stand before the Lord when he says, "What did you do with the Pastors and families I sent to you, and you sent them away?"

b. Not accused of riot: criminal charges/compliant [3]
c. Unruly: unsubdued, i.e. insubordinate (in fact or temper): KJV—disobedient that is not put under, unruly [4]

We see that the children are to be under the authority of their parents and they are to see to it that they are obedient children. When the children become young adults, they do become more accountable for their own choices and actions and the parents become less and less responsible for their actions. We do not always agree with our children's decision, but we do have to love and accept them. They will eventually have to come under the Lordship of Jesus Christ and bow their knee to Him alone.

A totally different matter is if you happen to be the Pastor and your adult children are in leadership position, but in moral sin. In I Samuel we see where Ely had his two sons in the priestly office, but his sons were immoral and extorted money from the people. They had no regard and desecrated the temple. We need to set the kids down when they are in sin and reprove them, just as we would anyone else. They are not untouchable. I would rather set them down for discipline purposes than see the Holy Spirit chastise them or the pastoral staff for allowing sin in the camp. That is a big price to pay. Beware! (I Sam 2:12-4:22 KJV)

4. The Bishop Must Be Blameless As a Steward of God

a. **Bishop:** a superintendent, i.e. Christian officer in genitive case charge of a (or the) church (literally or figuratively): KJV—bishop, overseer[5]
b. **Blameless:** unaccused, i.e. (by implication) irreproachable: above suspicion, guiltless [6]
c. **Steward:** a house-distributor (i.e. manager), or overseer, i.e. an employee in that capacity; by extension, a fiscal agent (treasurer); figuratively, a preacher (of the Gospel): KJV—chamberlain, governor, steward. (Custodian, keeper, guardian)[7]

The Bishop he must be someone who can be trusted with God's money and also budget the household money. Girls, please realize that the church money is not your money. One of the main reasons that a ministry will fail is poor management of funds. This brings a real reproach to the Gospel when it happens.

d. **Not self willed**: self-pleasing, i.e. arrogant: Headstrong, obstinate, stubborn, pig-headed, willful[8]
e. **Not Soon Angry**: irascible: KJV—soon angry. Touchy, testy, grumpy, quick tempered, hot tempered, short tempered[9]
f. **Not given to wine**: staying near wine, i.e. tippling (to drink alcoholic liquor habitually or excessively) (a toper) (somebody who drinks alcohol heavily and habitually: KJV—given to wine.[10]
g. **No Striker:** a smiter, i.e. pugnacious, Inclined to fight or be aggressive, confrontational, belligerent, argumentative; contentious (quarrelsome): KJV—striker.[11]
h. **Not given to filthy lucre:** (gain); sordid; KJV—given to (greedy of) filthy lucre.[12]

Filthy lucre is dishonest gain; this is when a preacher teaches or prophecies something that is not true just to get the dollars. Some preachers are not popular because they speak truth and do not compromise with the Word of God for filthy lucre. Whatever you neglect to preach to the flock is negligence, and it will be required at your hand at the Judgment Seat of Christ, especially if you intentionally stay away from certain subjects because of the fear of man. You should fear God more. Girls, encourage your husband not to be fearful of man!

I think these qualifications have a double-edged sword effect. If we indeed say that God has called us to pastor, then we ought to take it very seriously and always endeavor to come up higher to His standards. This is time not to make excuses for ourselves, but to cry out to God to help us to be changed into His likeness. The Word of God is our mirror. We look into it and are cleansed by the water of His Word.

Attributes of the Overseer

> **Fond of guests**, i.e. hospitable: KJV—given to (lover of, use) hospitality. Friendly, welcoming, and generous to guests or strangers[13]

Girls, this is one for you to monitor. Your home is supposedly your castle; at least some say it is your husband's castle. Now that you are in the ministry it can seem like it becomes everyone's place to come and dump on you. I do not believe this should happen. Years ago, when the pastors were overrun with people knocking on their door at all hours of the day and night, it seemed like many came right around supper time. The kids would have to take a back seat to these adults and their ill-mannered arrivals. Suppertime is when the family gathers around the table to enjoy each other after a busy day at school and the workplace. It is a time to reconnect, talk through issues and plan for the next day.

Girls, Set Your Boundaries

We have found over the years that some pastors have no boundaries whatsoever. They have allowed people to come into the privacy of their own home and make demands on their time, food supply, and family. This should not to be! We need to be able to keep fences in place so the people know when they have crossed over the line. I do not want that for my children. I want them to see the blessings of the ministry. I do not want to have my children go to their rooms every time someone comes to the house with a personal problem. This can cause a child to become resentful and bitter over the years, feeling that others are more important than they are. The subject of resentments preachers' kids have against the church and their parents will be addressed in another chapter. And the phone! Phone counseling should only take place during office hours. The phone has caused many misunderstandings and families have become embittered to those taking precious time from family members. There is also the matter of protecting our children from all the sorrows and pains of life. If we allow people to enter our lives at any given time and they bring their "baggage" with them, the children will think that is what ministry is all about.

Dennis and I have offices inside the church, and if there is any counseling to be done, it is done at the church. We practice regular office hours so that we can accommodate the needs of the people. If we keep a professional atmosphere in place then the congregation will think of us in that sense. We work hard in continuing education to present ourselves as educators and professionals. If we are too familiar with the people because they spend more than the normal amount of time in the pastor's home, they become critical of our humanness, frailties, and how we conduct our home life.

While I have said all this to explain boundaries, I do believe we should make our home hospitable to people. I took a survey of 100 people from various churches, and asked if the pastor's should entertain in their home. At least 80% did not think that it was necessary and that the pastor should be able to have his privacy. The rest (mainly leadership) would like to be in the pastor's home maybe once or twice a year, which is reasonable. If someone came to my house unexpectedly, I would not turn them away, but I also would suggest that they meet me at the church, so I can properly minister to the need of the person without household interruptions

My suggestion is to keep strong boundaries. Have people over because you want to entertain. Do not to discuss problems in the home, especially if you happen to have a family at home and are not an empty nester. The hurting people will also appreciate the privacy and professional atmosphere you provide for them. They will feel safety during their perplexity. I know sometimes this is not possible when someone comes battered and bruised in life, but try to spare the children as much as possible. When they see how loving and caring you are toward those who are hurting it will cause them to take up compassion as well.

> **Fond to do good**, i.e. a promoter of virtue; KJV—love of good men.[14]

The pastor and his wife need to be a lover and friend to the believers. They need to be glad to see them with open arms of communications. When talking about the Disciples of Christ, the Bible says you shall know them by their love. Too many times in a church setting, it is the pastor and his family against the church people. That is not exactly what Paul was talking about when he said if there are any differences between you, clear them up so that you will enjoy where the Lord has placed you. This will be your responsibility to see to it that you are a lover of the believers. Take steps to clear up any misunderstandings that have formed over the time in ministry. Some questions to ask yourself are:

- At times, we may move on to another church but the same problems still exist. You had thought if you could just go to another church you would not have this problem. If the same problem still exists, now you need to carry out an evaluation of your own heart.
- Who first offended you, how do you get to this place that the people are your enemy?
- Have you gone back over the times you were offended but did not forgive and forget?
- Was it easy for you to forgive but the wounds were deep and someone keeps ripping it open?
- Are you disappointed that the same problems have followed you even though you moved across the country?

Girls, Will You Pray with Me?

Dear Lord, I thought this battle would be over when I left the church or churches that have hurt and offended me. I thought I could start over with this new congregation who voted for me to be their new pastor. I found new hope when they said yes to me. They wanted me, and I was so happy that they saw value in me.

But Lord, now I am miserable. I left my house, and my children left their friends. I moved all this way to see that people are the same everywhere. I am disappointed in their behavior, and I am upset that the same problems are resurfacing.

Jesus, help me to look deep inside of my heart and identify the hurt and pain I am again experiencing. I do not want to be like this. I do not want to hurt my family by another move or failure. I cannot understand why your people are rude, mean, and do not love like the Bible commands. Give me the courage to see my part in this whole picture. Help me to see what I need to do to make this right. I know you have called me to preach the Gospel and to pastor, so please give me what I need to help this situation. I need people to pastor. What is it that repels them from me and me from them? Search me and know my heart. See if there is any wicked way in me, and I will be sure to repent of my sins and shortcomings.

Dear Jesus, as I look back over my pastoral history, I remember the time when ________________ hurt me. They superseded my pastoral authority and caused pain and sorrow in my family. I forgive them for hurting me. I ask you to forgive me for my part in this sin. Cleanse me from the sin and wounding __________caused in my life. I release that church and the people who offended me, betrayed me, used me, and lied about me. I release those who did not understand me, those who wanted a pastor to preach but did not want the pastor to have any authority.

Dear Pastor and Wife,

As you know, there can be many things that have caused you not to be a lover of the believers, so take quality time out. Deal with the hurts and pains of life and get this out of your hearts. The Lord knows how much you want to pastor and be in His complete, divine will. He knows how much you and your family have suffered at the hands of believers and that is a disgrace to the body of Christ.

Can you forgive them who hurt you, so you do not take your anger and fears out on this new body of believers? They want you, but they want you whole, without any of the excess baggage you carry from the wounding of your soul. Clear this up as soon as you can and God will bless you with new found, believing friends who will want to come up beside you and work with you in the ministry.

I can remember the time when we left one church; it was so hurtful to us that it put a horrific fear in my heart against the congregation. I thought that we were about to do a repeat of the last church. I would be so afraid of what the people would do or say to us. I lived this way for a period of time, but then I realized it was a pattern or cycle of pain. I had other ministers who were equipped with this type of healing to help me. It was a real relief to receive healing. I no longer reacted to fears and rejections. This was very healing even though I had to humble myself and begin to confess the areas I failed in; it set me and my husband free to love the people.

a. **Sober:** safe (sound) in mind, i.e. self-controlled (moderate as to opinion or passion): KJV—discreet, sober, temperate (self disciplined, moderate)[15]

I love the Scripture in II Timothy 1:7: *For God did not give us a spirit of timidity of cowardice, of craven and cringing and fawning fear, but (He has given us a spirit) of power and of love and of calm and well-balanced mind and discipline and self control.* The Amplified Bible

We understand that we have a responsibility to be sober in all things. We do not go off on tangents and are level-headed, seeking God in all things. This brings stability to the church and to your leadership abilities.

b. **Just:** equitable (in character or act); by implication, innocent, holy (absolutely or relatively): KJV—just, meet, right (-eous).[16]

Do not be biased or opinionated, but listen to both sides of an issue first so that you are not labeled that it can only be one way. Be known as a just man or woman of God so that people will be able to come, and you will have great discernment. If you are just, you are wise, and then you can be trusted with their lives.

There is nothing worse than the accusation that the man or woman of God is not fair and does not care for the people. Your reputation should be that people can come to you because you will not judge them, but lovingly treat them wisely and fairly. To do this, you must know what the Bible says about every issue they have. If you cannot decide right away, do not make a decision until you have prayed and found the answer in the Word of God and not that of your opinion.

c. **Holy:** which denotes formal consecration; and from, which relates to purity from defilement), i.e. hallowed (pious, sacred, sure):[17]

The Lord wants us to be living examples of his holiness. When the people see that we live clean, consecrated lives before God and the people, we will be modeling this. Too many times in this region of the country, the people talk about how they invited the minister or priest to a function where they became drunk and had to be taken home. Some ministers and priests have revoked driver's licenses due to drinking. This should not be spoken of you. Another example of this is when the pastor, elder, overseer, or bishop talks with impure words or actions. This is of the old life, and we are to put off the former conversation and unholy words. "Let no corrupt communication proceed out of your mouth, but that which is good to the use of edifying, that it may minister grace unto the hearers." (Eph. 4: 29 KJV)

d. **Temperate:** strong in a thing (masterful), i.e. (figuratively and reflexively) self-controlled (in appetite, etc.): KJV—temperate. [18]

Paul makes it plain by repeating this attribute; we are to master our emotions and control our appetites, whatever sort they may be.

People do things in excess and do not consider it wrong, but they have given their heart to another by not controlling what is in their power to control. This could be any good thing that has become an obsession instead of a tool to have fun (sports, shopping, work, family etc.)

e. Holding fast the faithful word he has been taught

The men and women of God should be able to discern and keep the Word of God in the forefront. We must not give in to new teachings that are questionable, but rather we must rely on the basic principles of doctrine. There will always be things which will try to draw you away. Do not be one who cannot discern what is of God from what is a distraction from where God has assigned you. It may not be bad, but if it takes you away from your assignment, it could be.

We must be careful of every new wind of doctrine or revival that comes along. These days you see it all on TV, and I find myself not wanting to have such a display of the flesh. Some statistics say if you are in the 45-60 year old age bracket, you take fewer chances in the ministry. I would rather think we are wiser, we have been around the block once or twice, and partook of some of the so-called "revival fires" that have wreaked havoc in the church instead of promoting healthy growth.

I have seen ministers drive a certain "move of God" into the ground until they literally had to shut the doors of the church. What is that about? I want to do things decently and in order, so that the people can hear the Word of God, which is the most important part of the church service. Don't get me wrong; we have excellent praise and worship, but then it is time for the Word of God to be preached or taught, since the preacher has hopefully spent many hours preparing for the feast. People are changed by hearing the Word and being obedient to the Word.

Too many people have camped at laughter, jerking, rolling, leaping, prophecy, and professional entertainment instead of worship. These things may have been good for a season, but just as the cloud moved when The Lord God Jehovah was ready for the Children of Israel to move on, the people also need to do this. The Israelites had a long journey ahead of them and no time to tabernacle/camp. God meant those times to be a temporary blessing, not for them to build a doctrine out of it. You will not find some of these manifestations in the Word. What do you do about that? Move on and preach sound doctrine.

f. That he may be able by sound doctrine both to exhort and to convince the gainsayers.

Study and be eager and do your utmost to present yourself to God approved (tested by trial), a workman who has no cause to be ashamed, correctly analyzing and accurately dividing, rightly handling and skillfully teaching the Word of Truth. (II Tim. 2:15 AMP)

The responsibility to know the Word of God and basic doctrines of the Bible is given to all pastors and their wives. We should be able to locate and explain each one of them. You need an understanding yourself so that you can lead the people in the way of righteousness. Sometimes pastors may get bored with doctrine. However, safety exists in knowing sound doctrine especially when the people have visited other churches with some strange teachings. It is a comfort to them that you know where it is found and you can intelligently (rightly divide) let them know that it is not scriptural. Since you are not their parent, you cannot simply get by with the words, "because I said so!" To my surprise, there are men of integrity who have these qualifications and others who do not, due to their past misfortune and failure as a Christian. However, they are in the ministry and they believe that the call is great in their life, no matter what lifestyle from which they have come. Some think that preaching supersedes character, to our shame. As the Word says, we are an open epistle read of all men. Our everyday lives preach louder than our words on Sunday morning.

What Was Your Husband Doing When The Call of God Came?

It is amazing to compare what different husbands were doing when the Call of God came upon them. Many had a secular career when their life's plans were interrupted and changed completely when the plan of God superseded their plan. It is awe-inspiring to hear the different stories of how the banker, engineer, drug addict, builder, alcoholic, and town hell raiser all ended up behind the pulpit. They were on their way somewhere when the Lord captured their heart and turned them around to do the work of the Lord.

When the husband said those dreaded words to his wife, "I am called to be a Pastor," it is no secret that some wives silently balked all the way to the altar of ordination or acceptance of the church pulpit. Maybe you wondered in bewilderment what you would do now. God called him, so what happens to our world as we know it? I did not sign up for this. I was happy as the wife of a doctor, attorney, or carpenter. I was just about to leave you since you were so wicked. Another was dying when God healed them, changing their life around so dramatically that he devoted the rest of his life to the gospel, leaving the wife wondering, "You are going to do *what*? How are we going to pay for this?" Some men leave six-figure income careers to minister the gospel and stand behind a pulpit, with a small congregation, and they not sorry to leave that career for the pastorate. It can throw a woman into shock.

This news has been great a disappointment to many parents as well as fiancées, newlywed and established wives. I remember what my dad said when we broke what we thought was good news to him. Not happy at all, he looked very intently into our eyes and said, "Now what do you want to go and do that for?" Not expecting a negative question, I was silenced. It was not until years later, before he died, that he told me that he was proud of me for devoting our lives to the Gospel of Jesus Christ.

The wife is wondering how she got there; how long this will last, as if it is just another hobby. This is confusing to her since she did not marry a preacher. She married a man with a career, with a pension, and with plans for security. Yes, we love God, but I did not want to take it this far. I am comfortable like it is. We can still serve God, but keep your day job!

You're Gonna Do What?

I asked some friends of mine how God called them, and I think you'll enjoy reading their stories.

Dennis and Sandy:

I remember it very well. It was just shortly after I met Sandy, my precious wife-to-be. We had just finished a Sunday night service at Jesus Christ Holiness Church, in Fort Dodge Iowa. It was not one of those stem winder services. Actually, I don't even remember what the message was that night. But, after church it was our custom to go down to the basement level of the church and raid the refrigerator, with the pastor's blessings of course. Sandy was busy getting out the sandwich meat and all the trimmings when all of a sudden the Holy Spirit spoke to my heart. I was just leaning against the counter in the kitchen and the Holy Spirit said, "Dennis, I want you to preach the Gospel." I was not thrown to the floor or left in tears. I just remember hearing Him speak to my heart in such a wonderful, quiet way. But it left a profound impression on me. As a matter of fact, a few days later, I found myself talking to one of my instructors at the community college about a change of career directions. You see, I was a student in a tech school for auto mechanics, and I knew God was speaking to me about the ministry. My instructor said to do whatever I felt was right but to consider finishing school and go into the ministry afterwards.

Well, after I graduated from auto mechanic school, I married this wonderful woman of God, Sandy, and then began to serve in the church, preparing for the ministry. We continued in that local church for a number of years, knowing we were preparing for the pastoral ministry.

A few years later, we attended Country Mission Bible School. We would travel about 75 miles one way each Monday night. I continued my secular job while serving in the local church and seeking the ministry. During this period of life, I also worked in a slaughter house and as an auto mechanic. At times I would work as a roofer and other kinds of laborer. Sandy and I both continued to seek God, study the Bible and prepare our hearts, as well as serve in whatever way possible in order to qualify ourselves for ministry. Yes, it would have been easier to go to school, but we did continue to grow in the Word and the Lord eventually promoted us time and time again. Over the years we were pastors of four churches: one Assembly of God and the rest independent churches. It has been a good ride, although rough at times, but we have wonderful stories to tell and miracles to pass on to others.

Dave and Kris:

It was 1980 when Dave was just transferred to Clear Lake, Iowa with Getty Oil. Within a year, he was the youngest manager in the company managing the largest propane branch in the corporation. We had arrived, after a very rocky six years of marriage, at what they considered the "ideal life." We had a beautiful home, two healthy children, a great church family and lots of healthy friendships, but things were about to change.

In the spring of 1982, I had a dream that we moved from Clear Lake for Dave to attend Bible School. I shared the dream with no one, but the next day Dave had an "earth shattering" word from the Lord that he was to go to Rhema for nine months and then go to Jefferson, Iowa his hometown. He came home that evening, visibly shaken, and with fear and trembling shared his experience with me. God had been so faithful to share the vision with both of us that even though the risk seemed high. Our families thought we were crazy, and we had no jobs or support system in Tulsa. We took off on what was to become one of the greatest adventures in our lives.

Fast forward 26 years. As I look back at that time, I can see the hand of God on us at every turn. We've had some agonizing experiences. We've felt the pain of betrayal, seen our children hurt, felt incredible financial, spiritual, and emotional pressure. More than once I have wanted to "throw in the towel" but God has been faithful, even when I haven't.

The good has outweighed the bad. Our church is full of three generation families, ours included. When I look across the front row of our sanctuary on Sunday mornings and see the seats filled with our children and grandchildren I am filled with gratitude. It doesn't get any better than this. Isn't that just like our God?

Tom and Stella:

I was called by God in a large Assembly of God church after an altar call. As everybody went down to the front to pray, I decided I would go down to the altar and started praying. As I was standing along the side of a wall, it was as though somebody had slapped me on the head. I looked around and no one was there, but I felt something like a fire start from top of my head down to the soles of my feet. It was burning on the inside of me like a charcoal briquette. I was totally consumed with the fire and light of God.

I went home that night and was not able to sleep; the Holy Spirit began to talk to me about my future ministry. I had no doubt that I was called into the ministry after that. I was not married at this time when the Lord was showing me what I would do for him. I was caught up in His glory. I spent much of my time alone after work, studying His Word and in prayer. It took me ten years to get into full-time ministry, and some of the things He impressed upon me are coming to pass thirty years later.

I was already called to preach the gospel when I met my wife. She was newly saved, and she has been my faithful companion all these years working in the ministry side by side.

It is very interesting of what conviction and what fervor some entered the ministry, the stories are endless and usually the fire burns within them still.

Chapter 3

Rejection is an Ugly Word

Rejection. What a dreadful word. I call it the Ugly Twin of Betrayal, since they join forces to cause untold heartache. You cannot have one without the other; they travel in pairs, and they are nasty partners in crime. A rejection hotline on the internet and all different types of self-help programs exist to help others cope with rejection. According to Wikipedia, the word "rejection" was first used in 1415 and the original meaning was "to throw" or "to throw back." Scores of songs have been written about rejection, and people can relate their own lives to the story heard in those lyrics.

I think I can safely say that most people have felt the sting of rejection at some point in their lives. It would be mundane and gloomy to go through all the ways someone may be rejected. Do me a favor: close your eyes and think about the last time you were rejected. *It hurts.* I find that when we experience the wounds of rejections while living the Christian life, we then may identify with His sufferings as well.

Girls, do you remember a time when you did not think you'd have to suffer for Christ? I do. I would read the Scriptures in I Peter, but evidently I did not believe them since some of the ministers we followed after were preaching something very different. It took me a season to realize that it did not matter what someone else taught; I was responsible for understanding and following what the Word of God said. (I would suffer with or without believing that part of the Word.) Oh, how silly we are at times to think we can dictate to the Lord what we will and will not accept. It is just a matter of time before we go through a fiery trail according to James 1:2-4. How could I have been wrong, thinking that I would not be affected by trials and suffering? This was nobody's fault other than my own for not searching the scripture daily to see what God's Word said.

Isaiah the Prophet wrote about Jesus in chapter 53, a chapter is very familiar to us as Pastors. "*He is despised and rejected of men; a man of sorrows, and acquainted with grief: and we hid as it were our faces from him; he was despised, and we esteemed him not. 4. Surely he hath borne our griefs, and carried our sorrows: yet we did esteem him stricken, smitten of God, and afflicted. 5. but he was wounded for our transgressions, he was bruised for our iniquities: the chastisement of our peace was upon him; and with his stripes we are healed.*" (Isaiah 53: 3-5)

I thank God for these beautiful Scriptures of His suffering for us; it says that Jesus was rejected of men. The Strongs Concordance defines rejection as "abandoned of men; deserted discarded, forsaken, dumped, neglected, cast off." To discover that we too would be rejected, it would be part of the package to accept the suffering Jesus, and our own suffering for him. When Jesus was in His ministry, there is overwhelming evidence that He was rejected. He told his disciples that the religious leaders of the day would eventually kill him. We can look at some incidents in Jesus' life and realize we suffer the same way! In Mark 8:34, when they saw Jesus coming into their region, they asked him not to come to their coast but pass on by.

They saw him cast the demons out of the man from Gergesenes (that was too much power for them.) It is the same way today: people want to know why you as a pastor insist upon doing things which make the people fearful or uncomfortable. They do not applaud you for the person who was set free, but criticize you for your method.

The church today is seeker-sensitive, and not Holy Spirit or Word-sensitive. This is like an epidemic. I recall an incident when we came into the town we have pastored for now seventeen years. A local pastor of the same denomination called and said we were not welcome to start a new church. My husband and I had already moved into the area and had a small church congregation of approximately 40 people. Needless to say, we left that organization for another, but we kept to the plan of God. Rejection is not just from the flock. Jesus suffered from the religious leaders of the day. They tried everything they could to destroy or discredit Him.

I went to a pastoral couples' picnic just last week, and I noticed that there were only three pastoral couples who have stood in the test of time. Many times we could have moved away in the midst of rejection and pain. However, when God gives you a mandate to build the church in a certain area, He also equips you with strength in Him to stand firmly when you feel like running.

In Mark 6:3, Jesus spoke the truth, and performed healings and miracles. The religious leaders were offended and asked of him, "who do you think you are," "where do you get your authority," and "we know you are just the carpenter's son." The same circumstances happen to pastors as well. I particularly love this one: "Who gave you authority to preach, given that you are a woman?" Jesus would answer "my Father," and I answer "my heavenly Father and my husband." That usually either quiets them, or they find a new place to worship. In Luke 4:28, despite all the miracles and good, the scribes and Pharisees, filled with wrath, picked apart his ministry. How can this be when we do some great things for Jesus, that the people can be mad or try to dictate how to do it differently?

Let's now take a look at **Rejection**. When we search the Scriptures to determine how Jesus was rejected, we find certain buzz words.

In Mark, they were "offended" with him. They stumbled over his words, and had great displeasure in him.

In Luke, their anger was so strong they became filled with wrath and indignation. They refused to listen to him.

In John, Jesus' own relatives disowned him. They rejected him and did not receive his words.

Now let's talk about us as servants of God. Jesus said in this world we would have tribulation, and he sure was right. Yet, He also said that he would pray for us. I know that most pastors and we wives go through this type of suffering from time to time. If you say you go through it all the time, I would wonder, girls, if you were in the wrong profession.

- 80% of pastors and 85 % of their spouses feel discouraged in their roles.
- 90 % of pastors said the hardest thing about ministry is uncooperative people.[19]

I know we have had seasons of rejections for various reasons, some of our own makings and others due to a problem inside the church that will not be remedied until confrontation takes place. I do not like confrontation. I have to fast and pray before we confront. Girls, this is when I love my husband to be my leader, pastor, husband, head of the house, priest of the home, provider, protector, bread winner and whatever other names have been put on him.

Let me remind you something about myself: I grew up a tomboy. My father was a drill sergeant in the U. S. Army, and when he came home from WWII we became his little army. I was the rough 'n tough girl who could whip most boys. I loved to physically fight. Now I am suddenly supposed to be all grown up and a loving, caring pastor's wife? Wow! People expect you to be sweet and passive while they treat you as they please. How can you do that when people are saying things about you that are not true? They do not understand you nor do they care to. Often they think I should have my feelings in check and be the doormat as they tell me what they think of me on the way out the door! Not so easy when that rough 'n tumble tomboy is still deep inside of me.

I have learned many things, since I came into the pastorate more than 31 years ago. This is undeniable: I hope I am not the same person I was when we first began. I realized there were times that I would suffer, but it was because of my own selfishness and anger. There is no reward in that. I also realized there are times when I could rest in Christ and have an answer accompanied by the Fruit of the Spirit so I would not have suffered for anything less than the Glory of God. Oh, how sweet it is that when you are reviled, you revile not. The Lord takes note of suffering, and he alone can bring peace and joy into your heart at times of strong dilemmas. People will want to know why you are not upset, and you can teach them with meekness.

Girls, over the years I have heard the unbelievable stories of confrontation of pastors and their wives. Many of them have not been pleasant, and when I heard the pastor's side I felt empathy for him/her. Likewise, I have heard horror stories of how a pastor or wife has hurt one of the sheep severely with a tongue lashing, black balling, or just ignoring the person until they left the church.

The Scruffy Moustache

We have an odd story of our own. We had taken a new pastorate and spent two to three years with this fussy old congregation. Nothing pleased them. We went on a family vacation, and I had asked my husband if he would try and grow a mustache while we were away. Nothing wrong with that, right Girls? We thought it was a personal and harmless decision. Two weeks later, he had this scruffy outgrowth under his nose.

Dennis prepared for Sunday morning service, donning his three-piece suit, crisp white shirt, matching tie and polished shoes. He shyly walked out with his new addition, a scruffy new mustache, of which we both were proud. It was a small service that day, with only a handful of people that would make any young pastor discouraged. We greeted the people as if they were the King and Queen of England. Then it happened. Dennis got up to open the service, and the woman made her calculated move. As soon as he opened His Bible, she stood up, loudly declaring, "If he is too lazy to shave in the morning, he's too lazy to pastor! I will not listen to a lazy man!" She marched her husband and adult daughter out the door. I just happened to be in the back hoping to greet some latecomers. She stopped by me and with a scornful look on her face and in a tone that would make anyone tremble, "If he is too lazy to shave, he's too lazy to be the pastor!"

Dennis was devastated and confused to think that people would become so angry over a mustache. Now, do you think that should cause an exodus on a Sunday morning? Waves of rejection slapped both of us as we tried to finish the service. When this happens, fear overwhelms you. It is hard to explain unless you have been there yourself. The young preacher finished the service, immediately went back home and shaved.

Somehow God gave me the ability to not get mad and disregard these people. No one needs to be controlled or treated the way this couple tried to do to us. I went to their house and tried to reason with them, letting them know that he was in the process of shaving. That day we swallowed every ounce of pride we had, which was not much. We had been so beaten down by these very few people, we did not know how much more we could take. At that time and early in our ministry, we bowed to people and what they thought. We did not have much confidence in our leadership abilities. We spent much time in prayer trying to understand our role as pastor. I know God honored us by watching and waiting to see how we would react to these people. We passed a test that day not knowing that God would have the last say in the matter, and He did. It was not long after when they realized that their regime was over in the church and the Holy Spirit would now be in charge. They left the church and it began to finally grow.

I know I have hurt people along the way. Some, I was really mad at. Some, I did out of pure ignorance, which is not an excuse, but rather sin. I am truly sorry for the people I have hurt; they have found other shepherds who hopefully loved them more than I could.

Rejection is Nasty

Rejection is a nasty thing. When you are being rejected, you may want to rise up to fight, or you may want to retreat to lick your wounds. No one wants to be rejected, or at the least they want to reject you before you reject them. What a battle of emotions! This is what Jesus went through, but he did not fight back like we may do today. Oftentimes we feel that if we do not let them know how we feel, they have won. They may have said awful words to you, cursed you, and lied about you. God is the one that is keeping score. He will repay especially if they do not repent. This is what the Word says about rejection:

- Mark 6:3; they will be **offended** with you.
- They will **stumble** over the words you spoke, preached, or taught.

- Luke 4:28 they will take **great displeasure** in your word or actions.
- Luke 23:18; they would **not listen** to truth.
- They will be very **angry and unreasonable** even if you can prove it in the Bible.
- The nicest people will be filled with **wrath and indignation.**
- They will **refuse to listen** to you they will not receive your words; they will quit listening to you before you ever quit talking. They have shut down, communication breakdown.
- John 1:11; they will **disown** you.
- They are **not teachable.**

This continued rejection of people wears on our spiritual leader's heart and mind. It penetrates into our family life and leaves a bitter taste in the lives of our children. I know we wanted to be in it for a lifetime, but in today's world, many Pastors leave the ministry each year. What a tragic thing, to think that they were once young couples full of love for God and people, but now are reduced to leaving the ministry. Some men leave because the wife has made the ultimatum "Choose between the church and the family. You cannot have both!"

FACT:

- Over 50% of pastor's wives feel that their husbands entering ministry was the most destructive thing to ever happen to their families.[20]

DO THE MATH:

- 1500 pastors leave the ministry permanently each month in America
- 7,000 churches close each year in America
- 4,000 new churches start each year in America
- 50% of pastors' marriages end in divorce
- 70% of pastors continually battle depression[21]

Words are so hard to take back. Numerous times I have been on the other side of a counseling session where the person grieves or reacts to the words that have been spoken to them. It does not matter if it is the pastor, his wife, their children, a board member, etc. It all hurts unless you are the type of person that loves to engage in debate and confrontation. Yes, there are people who find it fun and rewarding to be able to have the best argument so they can win. It's all about winning, and they never consider the cost of hurting or losing a brother or sister in the Lord. This type of person may have been rejected all their life and this makes them want to be right at any cost. Conversely, they may be the type of person who has always had it their own way. They are not team players, and they end up hurting others with their rejection by words and actions.

No Place to Go

Some people relive the pain of childhood. The times a parent had harshly treated them or spoke words that damaged them for their adult life. They may have not been able to recover from those words or treatment. I remember a time we ministered at a mission center; many were preachers' children who were hooked on some form of drug to numb the pain of their childhood. This was a divine set-up for the preacher's son who listened intently to what Dennis had taught that day.

My husband is a very kind father figure, and on that day he taught on bitterness and unforgiveness. The lesson greatly touched one man who was in his mid-thirties. Later, in the privacy of this man's room, Dennis knelt down beside him. He asked him if he could repent over all the things his dad and other men had put him through since he was a preacher's son. The man fell into Dennis' arms, and wept from the depth of his soul for a very long time. The years of rejection had worn down this man; he had nothing left but a free place to stay at the mission, in the middle of a Michigan forest. He had no other place to go but on his knees. This preacher's son had a divine appointment with God to clear his heart of all unforgiveness and bitterness, so he could move on with his life and be healed inside out.

Rejection is an Ugly Enemy

Rejection is such an ugly enemy. Many times you may perceive rejection when no one is trying to reject you. It may not be in anyone's heart to deliberately reject you, and you could be your own worse enemy. You have been rejected so many times that you know the routine. You could walk in the middle of a group of fine church people and think that they are talking about you just because they happened to laugh or look up when you entered their area. It is usually the furthest thing from the truth, but the devil loves to make you think that they are against you. If we could only make people understand that they are loved and accepted. When they feel rejected, most often they will isolate themselves wanting nothing to do with people who they think do not like them or accept them. The enemy loves to play tricks on our emotions.

A different matter which often occurs with people, who carry rejection, is that they will want to reject you before you reject them. What a vicious cycle in which you shoot yourself in the foot even though what you feel is not even true. As a pastor's wife it amazes me that people want to tell me what they think I am like. They want to inform me that they know why I do not like them and reject them. Over the years I have become bold in my approach concerning these types of statements. I let them know if they are wrong or that I am just doing my job. I will apologize for what they may think I have done to them, since I truly did not mean to offend or hurt anyone. Many times they want to consume my time by putting me on the defense since it is a surprise to me that they even thought I rejected them. No one knows the heart of another like Jesus does.

Have you experienced any of these situations as a pastor's wife?

- They begin to name your attributes and what you think are your strong points. Now all of those things have become their source of contention. Who do you please, man or God? I choose God.
- They now want to engage you in their emotional rejection of you.

- They now want you to know how uncomfortable they are with you.
- It is as if they want to put a monitor on you, so you do not say or do anything that would cause them to feel rejected.

Sad to say, but you will always have "regulators" in your church who try to control the pastors or the way the church is growing. This is something to pray through. Try to understand their viewpoint, since it may hinder the growth of the church, the sheep, and the individual. We cannot give in to that spirit of rejection. In some ways it has a death grip of fear and control. The people will not want to see change; or if they do, it must be their way. Otherwise, they will feel abused and rejected. This can be a very strong spirit which can come in different mannerisms: meek, quiet, bold, accusatory, threatening, manipulative, but rejection nevertheless.

Girls, Beware of This

Rejection is something every pastoral couple needs to examine their hearts for at various times. Girls, we know when we become overly tired when we have not had proper time in prayer, devotion or family time. We ourselves can have a battle with rejection, especially if we have been wounded by rejection before. It is up to us to recognize the influence in our own lives so we do not operate under its sway. We need to stop what we are doing and spend some quality time with the Lord, cleansing ourselves in the water of the Word. We need to denounce all connections with rejection. Frequently, we may not realize the work load we have until we are tired and reacting to old wounds. This is not good, and we need to balance our life so that we know the familiar signs of rejection. Then it's time to back away for rest and relaxation.

Sometimes as pastors' wives and pastors we expect rejection from people on account of past experiences. We may have been hurt by leadership, or we may have not been able to keep the people for any type of longevity. We silently wait for them to tell us they are leaving, that they changed their mind about our leadership abilities. We expect it is coming soon, so we digress into a fearful expectation that they will leave, although most people have no intentions of leaving you. They love how you preach, teach and shepherd your flock. Nevertheless, the past has preconditioned you. This is very hard to handle, and we can scare them away by our attitudes and fears.

Our best weapon in this case is to love the people! Do not be afraid of them love on them. If they leave, then realize that God will replace them with others if we are truly called to pastor. He will bring the sheep. It is good to have a reserve of the Word built up in us and begin to rehearse what the Lord said about his church. His Word will give us strength and comfort.

Girls, Will You Please Pray With Me?

Dear Father God, I ask you in the name of Jesus to help me be healed of the sting of rejection. I have labored for you and the church, but I feel unaccepted and unappreciated. I feel they have taken my leadership ability and trampled on it. I feel they have something negative to say whatever I do. I feel like I have been abused and bitten by the sheep! They question everything I do. They try to nose their way into my personal family life. Nothing is private or sacred to them. Father, I feel like I have been battered and bruised by the people. I feel like they do not accept me for myself, and that I have to be formed into their image instead of the image of Christ. I feel like a failure and a slave in the eyes of the people.

I realize, Father God, that the enemy has come into my life, my heart, and my feelings. I realize that it is not all the sheep's problem, but it is me standing in the need of prayer. I realize that my heart has been hurt, and I have allowed the enemy of my soul to overwhelm me with untruths, bitterness and unforgiveness. I realize that my heart may have been hurt long before I entered the ministry and the hurts of the present have brought up unresolved issues of the past. I ask you to forgive me for harboring unforgiveness of the past that keeps me weak and vulnerable to the present. This has been an open door for the enemy to traffic in my life, and I refuse to allow him to take the joy out of the Call you have on my life.

Please Lord, let me make peace with my past and present so I can have a future pleasing you and caring for your sheep. I ask you to reveal to me those of my past who I need to forgive. I ask you to wash me clean of all old grievance of the past so I can be free to live in the present and take care of the problems of the day. I do not want to react to the people because of past. I want to face every challenge and be able to be part of the solution instead of the part of the conflict. I need your grace and freedom in my life to be able to minister effectively.

Now Lord, I forgive those who have hurt me in the ministry, and release them from any debt they owe me. I ask you to bless them and teach them your loving ways. Thank you for healing me from the pains of rejection, and even though rejection may come again, the slate of the past is clean. I will be able to deal with what the day brings because I have learned to lean into you and operate out of your Agape love and not out of the hurts of the past. The past is clear of any unforgiveness. Thank you for your great love for me that you would correct me.

In your son's name I pray. Amen.

Chapter 4

Betrayal is an Ugly Twin to Rejection

Betrayal is all together too familiar for pastors. Especially for the pastor's wife, since women process their feelings in a distinctly different way than men. I'm not saying that men do not hurt; they just seem to process it in different ways, like being angry or suppressing their emotions. I can tell when my husband is upset. His "halo language" speaks much louder than words. For example, if he's upset when it's time to set the table, he may begin to toss the dishes instead of placing them. Sometimes I joke, "Move away from the table and no one will get hurt." We ladies may have to talk about it. Sometimes it is blown out of proportion and other times it becomes a wound or hurt that they carry for a long time. The wound may cause us not to trust others, and we respond to them according to the last person who betrayed or hurt us.

Betrayal is an ugly word. It happens on all levels; it does not matter if you're a pastor of twenty or two thousand. It shoots a shot-gun blast wound in our soul. We live with these wounds for a long time; eventually, they can shape our personality. Often we will erupt with anger, usually unexpectedly.

I am reminded of the experience Jesus had in the Garden of Gethsemane, where he went through his hour of betrayal. We only think it began in the garden, when actually it began when he entered his ministry. One by one, his family members thought he was crazy or beside himself. The family, the mother, his brothers and sisters were looking on with the rest of the people, insinuating that he was now different. He went too far in these outrageous teachings, and they wanted to take him home. "Is this not Jesus, the carpenter's son?" (Mark 3:21; Matt. 12:46 KJV) We have heard the rumors about Joseph and Mary years before, and now he is saying that he is the Son of God!" Jesus was raised in the community; they went to synagogue together, played together, and enjoyed the feasts together.

Everything changed one day when Jesus went into his public ministry. He took his stand and boldness came upon him where he could say and demonstrate that "*the Spirit of the Lord is upon me, because he hath anointed me to preach the gospel to the poor; he hath sent me to heal the brokenhearted, to preach deliverance to the captives, and recovering of sight to the blind, to set at liberty them that are bruised, to preach the acceptable year of the Lord.*" (Luke 4:18-19 KJV) This was after the declaration from the heavens when he went to be baptized. Jesus went as called, but John looked at him and said "Oh, I am not worthy to even unlatch your shoe, let alone call you into repentance." John knew who Jesus was; they were cousins, raised together. Now he was coming for water baptism.

Jesus humbled himself there and was baptized. We know the account, that out of heaven, Father God confirmed His son, saying, ". . .This is my beloved son, in whom I am well pleased." (Matt. 3:17 KJV) From that time onward, Jesus declared his ministry to all and went about doing good and healing all that were sick and oppressed, for God was with him.

We see in the Gospels that others came against Him. The religious leaders of the day had something to say about him. "He is mad, he blasphemes, and he breaks the Jewish laws and traditions. Is this not the son of Joseph?" (Luke 5:21; Mark 2:17; Matthew 9:3 KJV) In the later parts of the Gospels, we see where even the disciples were wondering about Jesus. Here he was, saying some really off-the-wall things, like, "*I am going to die but be raised up on the third day*" and "*I have to die so you can live.*" Things they did not understand, yet they loved him and trusted him, somewhat. He was their Messiah come in the flesh, and now he says he is going to die? They were thinking, "Oh please, this is not what I signed up for; I was expecting you to take over this government, and we would rule and reign with you." (Matthew 16:21-28 KJV)

And These are His Disciples, His Close Friends?

At the time of Jesus' death, they gathered for one last supper before the ultimate betrayal. Confusion clouded their minds as they did not understand who would betray their beloved friend. I can hear the questions in the minds of the faithful disciples, the same questions we would ask if our pastor would be talking like that. "Are you feeling all right? Did you have a bad night sleep? Has something happened that we are not aware of that would bring you to such thoughts of death and betrayal? Do you need to go away for a rest? We know the people have been pressing you hard." Those are just the surface questions we begin with and then move on to more difficult ones. Jesus understood the disciple's confusion. Once again, Jesus said there was someone among them who would betray him, and he would die. Well, let us get this matter cleared up right now. Peter thought this was ridiculous. When Peter took it upon himself to correct this negative thinking pattern in Jesus, he was immediately rebuked, then he was told that he, too, would betray Jesus. Oh, now it was getting way out of hand. Peter knew he stood rock solid with Jesus. He was the one who had the revelation of Jesus, and the church would be built upon Him. How could he think of such a thing? How could he bring such hurtful accusation against Peter?

I Learned This the Hard Way

We do not understand what is beyond the bend; we live in a world of now. Many times, we have not taken the time to inquire of the Lord what information he wants us to have at this time. Therefore, things come at us in crisis force, hitting us with winds of adversity that the strongest Christian leaders would be blown over by, wind gusts of hurricane proportions. I have heard some say, "I did not know what hit me; I was not prepared for what happened to our family. It took me by surprise." Boy, did I learn that the hard way. The heart is wicked and only God knows our intent. (Jeremiah 17:9 KJV)

The only one in history who was not taken by surprise was Jesus. We realize through Scripture (Rev. 5:9 and Rev. 13:8) that before the very foundation of the world, Jesus was to be the slain Lamb of God who took the sins of the world upon him. This was the Plan. He was prepared. Mission accomplished.

Not so with us as Christian leaders. Many times we become excited about "The Call," whether or not we are actually called to be a pastor. We can get our own little rush preaching the Gospel to a congregation. This is *my* audience, *my* flock. They have to listen to me, *God said so*. How naïve we have been as leaders. Especially Charismatic leaders who take it up a notch, and say, "God said so, therefore follow after me." That may be harsh statement, but since I am a Pentecostal, Charismatic, Holy Ghost-filled preacher, I can pick on us. I am one of you! I do believe in hearing and obeying the voice of the Holy Spirit. Personally, I think that we have used this cliché to preface what we know is right, or what we want to do next in the church. We want the backing of the people so we say, "God said."

Why do we use such words? Are we fearful and insecure that they may not follow an idea of our own? If God said it, where is the evidence? Was it a successful campaign? Did you see the fruit of the ministry? Will they mark you as a false teacher or prophet?

As long as the healings, miracles, and prophecies come to pass, people will be with you. People are with us for various reasons; some we know about, some, we do not. If you have any insecurity whatsoever, it can make you concerned for your future. However, when the church hits a season of drought, for whatever reason (burn out, family problems, financial insufficiency, disgruntled people, etc.) the tendency is to look toward the pastors. We all know the old saying "the buck stops here." At times this can send the pastor's family into a tailspin. It has happened before, and now it is happening again. Suddenly a great tormenting fear beats down upon the pastor's mind.

Yea, Mine Own Familiar Friend, in Whom I Trusted . . .

Here is this once gracious congregation: friends of the family, comrades in arms, those that you broke bread with, and stayed up with in the hospital when a loved one was in danger. "Even my best friend has turned against me—a man I completely trusted; how often we ate together." (Psalms 41:9 LVB) You were at the births, graduations, weddings, and deaths of family members. People with whom that you shared your hopes and dreams, and supporters who said "Let's do it", now they are estranged. They have taken sides. It is easier to get rid of a pastor and his family than to let the entire church go down due to one person.

Oh my, we have much to explain to God before His White Throne Judgment Seat. What will be our defense when He asks, "Why did you fire my servant, whom I sent to you?" "What happened to the man of God and his family once you rejected them?" And of course the dreaded question that the Lord will ask His five-fold ministry, "How did you love and respond to the people I sent along side you, to help you grow in the ministry?"

This I know: while Jesus was being tried in the court, the disciples were no where to be found. The angry, accusing crowd was too much for them, so they hid themselves. Even when Peter came close, and they recognized him as one of the followers of Jesus, he crumbled under the fear of being punished for associating with such a blasphemer. I know I would have been afraid too. You either go along with the crowd, or you go into hiding.

I remember pastoring in a small town in Iowa. We were the last hope for that particular church. Several pastors failed over the previous fifteen years in this small farming community. We had heard the stories: some left in the middle of the night; some without a word to the board. Wounded and disheartened, they left not just the church, but the ministry.

At this time, we were quite young in the ministry. We thought we could tackle anything that came our way. After all, we knew we could do all things by Christ's strength. We had confidence in God's Call upon our lives, and we were so zealous to do His work. We just wanted to pastor.

Pastor we did. If anyone would have told us back then what we would go through, we would have chosen the evangelistic field! Even then, we would have to put up with wounded pastors and perhaps a controlling board. We were naïve and young. The church we grew up in loved and accepted us; they thought we were the best things since sliced bread. I had no idea that the other parts of the Body of Christ would not treat us with the same love and respect as where we grew up. No wonder some churches have selected a board of family members and trusted friends!

These people questioned everything we did. They set up surprise visits from our superintendent and district presbyter. The things I learned about myself were mostly through the accusations of the saints! I had no idea! The way I acted was normal to me. Yes, I did have to change in many areas. No, it was not all the church's fault. I had flaws, which were not apparent to me until someone started stepping on my toes and pointing the accusing finger at my husband and children. This is when the claws came out. Watch out when this begins to happen! You are now in a test, and the answer is not in the way you were raised to respond to people out of your anger, hurt, frustration and pain. The answer is in the Word of God.

For the next several years, I was in a testing ground, whether by people, the devil or my own sinful responses. I knew I had to change and line up with the Word of God. It was not going to be an easy task, but had to be done.

I was Lying in Bed, the Covers up to My Eyes

Did I mention that when we agreed to take over this church the people had no choice? We were the "last a ditch effort" from headquarters. If we could not make it, the church would be shut down. The church had a membership of thirteen people, in ages ranging from 45 to upper 60's. These long time members had the attitude, "We are the bosses. You are the hired preacher." When we began to pastor this little congregation, I was never so scared in all my life.

These people were unpredictable in their behavior. One day they would show us brotherly affection, and the next day, they darkened the door with a scowl on their faces. It got so bad that I did not want to get out of bed on Sunday morning. And that's a little difficult when you live in the apartment attached to the church!

I remember one day so plainly, even though it took place back in 1978. My husband is kind and gentle in nature, but very strong and determined in his pastoral office. I was lying in bed covers up to my eyes when he came in and questioned me as to why I was not ready for church. I told him I was not going because the people scared me. Without hesitation, he said, "You get out of bed, get dressed and stand at the entrance of the church. When they come in, you shake their hands, and look them in the eye, and say, 'I love you'."

To this day, I wondered why I listened to him. Maybe it was because I did not have a better plan. But I knew he would not think that one up on his own, since he did not like any type of confrontation in those days. So, I got up and did what he said. I stood by that door, reached my hand out to them, and said those words, "I love you." After a while, I actually did love them. Learning that I could care for those who did not care for me was a great life lesson.

About three months later, the people eventually realized we were serious about staying and loving them. The district counsel supported us, but the people left us. Only one man stayed, and from there we built the house of God. During the tenth year, we were feeling great success and stirring in the church, all at the same time. Sometimes, when this happens, you reach for the success and put aside those feelings that something is not quite right. We were so busy and excited that we failed to listen to the Holy Spirit trying to warn us of an oncoming battle. We ignored the prompting and continued to literally build the church.

When Did You Stop Loving Me?

We stayed in that church for eleven years, when to our dismay, circumstances began to change. We began to hear insinuations concerning the conduct of our two children. They seemed fine to us, as if we would notice anything about them. We had taken on a building project with church members. Soon it dwindled away to very few faithful members working on the project, and our shoulders bore the brunt of the workload. We devoted more time due the necessity of the church building, rather than to our children. Finishing the job became the driving force in our life at the time. We wanted to get it done.

The people were dissatisfied with us for various reasons. A new man was on the scene, and they wanted a pastor just like him. I still make people laugh when I share that I told a fellow minister, "I do not even know what a Benny Hinn is!" To my surprise, this Benny Hinn was a great preacher. They wanted us to be like him with all the miracles, gifts, you name it! Oh dear, it was not our call to be a Benny Hinn; we knew we could not work that up in us.

If I only had known what I know today, we would have been spared much heartache and pain when it came to raising our children. The devil does not play fair; he will take the most precious possessions around you and try to destroy them. To our dismay, it went down hill from there. We discovered we were the topic of a (secret) women's prayer meeting. Ouch! Lies were spoken about our children, although our children created enough sensation of their own to cause any board to freak out. I was devastated by all the talk, which nearly killed my soul. I could not understand how these once loving people could be so filled with animosity and hatred toward us. Many questions tormented my soul on a recurring basis:

- When did you stop loving me?
- Have I done any wrong that you have not done in your own parenting?
- Do you reject our family because my kids are in trouble?
- We have been with you this long, do you still not know our hearts?
- Did we fail to teach you how to love people and not condemn?
- Why do you want to throw us away?

We were heartbroken and angry. Life was over as we knew it. Our lives were turned upside down, and we did not know what to do. We were clueless, and it did not seem to matter to the people that we were hurting.

It was as if They Ripped My Heart Out

Our hearts ached like someone ripped them out and stomped on them. I did not know how to pick up the pieces. We could hear only one accusation at a time. The one that was the loudest was, "You are a lousy parent." We always thought we were very good parents. We made a pact when we first got married that our children would not walk in the ways of our fathers. Their words haunted my mind, "If you cannot have control over your own family, you do not deserve to be our pastors."

The mental anguish and torment of losing our children for a time to the world took a toll on us. The ridiculous accusations were spoken by the same people into whom we poured our time, abilities, and love. We had been too busy, literally building the church and following our dream. We thought everyone was "with us" in this endeavor.

When Jesus said that we would be betrayed and suffer as he did, I thought, 'this would not happen to me.' I confessed those things away, saying, "I am the righteousness of Christ Jesus; I am beyond the devil messing in my life." The sad truth sunk in that, yes, we would suffer with him, in order to rule and reign with him. (II Tim. 2: 11-13 KJV) I bowed my knee to the Lord Jesus Christ. The devil meant to destroy my family and remove us from of ministry. It is too much to speak or even write about. When we left the small town where we had raised our children, it was like a death. We mourned, grieved, and were angry over what had happened to our nice little family.

Where Did All the Leaders of Tomorrow Go?

We were very upset with the reproach and stigma it left on the church, but more importantly, how it affected the young men and women of the church. Judgment will come if the guilty do not repent. I know they scattered, but I do not know if they actually went back to church after that. What a waste of beautiful young men and women who could make a great difference in the community by being a Christian influences. The town's people saw the whole thing; it was juicy gossip. They could not understand why the church would reject the pastors in that fashion. That church has never prospered or grown since they rejected the family God had assigned to that town.

I learned something from a wise preacher. When you are having a problem in a church, it is usually only 5-10% of the people who are in disagreement with the leadership. The rest are just followers who are not involved and do not know the whole story. They love you but do not know what to do. We came to this knowledge after the fact, and it brought much healing to us. I know that the times we were alone and deserted, other members in the Body of Christ prayed for us. They carried us on the wings of prayer, and we made it through some very dark days of wrestling with the Call of God. We questioned if we were qualified to ever pastor a church again. There were times we could not pray at all; we just lay in the bed of mourning and cried ourselves to sleep. We knew others were praying when we had no prayer of our own except, "Help us, God."

I thank God for our brother and sister who invited us to rest and be restored in their church. They did not demand anything of the office we carried, but just let us weep as we sat on the front row. Their people comforted us by being sweet to us and not asking any questions or making any judgments. We felt safe. Thanks Dave, Kris and Agape Christian Family Church.

It's Hard to Heal a Heart That Has Been Stomped On

Our hearts were so betrayed they were hard to heal. Just when we thought we were mending, a fear would rush over us and again we would go through a rough time of rejection, fear, and bitterness. There is not one thing I would offer as consolation to the effects of betrayal except for Jesus. He died amid betrayal, but rose again to use it against the wiles of the devil and to save men from his grasp. I have an idea how many of you girls feel or have felt in some point in your life. It took time to get through the process of healing or even wanting to pastor again. I remember letting Dennis know one cold January day, that maybe one day, I would go back into the pastorate with him. He just cried.

Dennis and I were each other's comfort. No one understood our pain. I remember asking the presbyter where we could get help for our family. They had nothing to offer in the way of counsel for the wounded pastor. I was greatly disappointed and affected by the situation that I now have my own ministry to bring healing to wounded pastors and their wives.

For a long time, I grieved and mourned over my children. I carried that grief within my soul. I had lost the ability to laugh and smile. I enjoyed nothing. One day Dennis and I were driving down the street when he put his hand on my chest and commanded a spirit of grief to come off me. From that time on, I had strength to fight the battle instead of succumbing to the defeat of the battle over my soul and family. I recall when a pastor friend said that she was amazed at our resilience. I took it as a compliment but realized sometime later that I was still wounded. After a period of time, we started a church and went back into the pastorate. It was a different place, with new hopes and dreams and a heart to shepherd God's sheep, but the same wounding remained.

It did not take long to realize that by our response to people and situations, we were still wounded. Our trust level in God and people were very low. When trials came, we responded out of fear of being rejected again. Girls, this was extremely stressful to me and my husband. What used to be second nature to us was now terrifying. The overwhelming fear of what might happen to our life as we knew it kicked in. Would they reject us and walk away from us? Would they betray us as those before? Yes, they would, but now we are tough, we have been through a battle, and we knew how to fight. We prayed much but still did not seem to get any relief we needed to survive. I realized I was in trouble. This was my CALL; I did not have anything else to do for the Lord, but what He called me to do. When we cried out to the Lord in desperation we realized that if we did not get the help we needed from the Lord, we would not make it. He was faithful to send to us the messenger at the right time to begin the healing process. I am so grateful that He loves and cares for us.

- 590, or 57%, said they would leave if they had a better place to go, including secular work
- 935, or 89%, of the pastors surveyed also considered leaving the ministry at one time.[22]

Divine Appointment

A musical evangelist came through our church one day. Prior to that visit, I had not especially cared for his ministry. In the past, he would sing a few loud songs, collect a paycheck and be on his merry way. I let my husband know that I did not want him to come, since I would have to "clean up" after him. Part of my unspoken job description as a pastor's wife to hear the complaints and fix them if possible. The people would complain of the loud music and his attitude, and I was expected to make it all better.

Already hurting and fearful of people, I felt I was in a precarious place. Nonetheless, he came and ministered in a way he never had before. He began by preaching about Father God's love, and healing of the wounded heart. Taken by surprise, I sat weeping in the front row. He looked at my husband, pointed his finger at him, and said "You need to love and protect your wife." I was shocked! No one ever said that to Dennis before, and no one ever said that about me. He did not sing this time, even though he tried. This was a divine appointment for Dennis and me to hear about healing of our wounded hearts.

I literally ran after him when the service was over, as he was packing up. I said, "Whatever happened to you needs to happen to me!" He told me of how he met a ministry couple by the name of Jack and Tricia Frost, founders of Shiloh Place Ministry. Well, I went right home on a Sunday afternoon and called them. I spoke to Tricia and said, "Whatever you did for this guy, I need it done for me." She informed me that the next scheduled seminar was full, but she would call back if space opened. Well, do you know a space miraculously came available for us? We dropped everything and went out to Myrtle Beach. Jack and his team began to share their stories of how they were hurt in their lives and how God healed the wounds in their soul.

We began the seminar with guarded hearts, but the more we listened, the more we realized that this was a new truth of the Word of God. I had never thought about Father God. I only mentioned His name briefly to pray to Jesus. I became acquainted with what the Bible taught about Father God. I realized I had missed out on one third of the Trinity. What water on a dry and thirsty land! My soul accepted His gracious love which transformed and healed this wounded heart.

Long Journey of Healing a Broken Heart

What began was a journey of healing our broken hearts and understanding Father God's love for us. I had to take a close look at myself, and my responses to various situations over the years. I had been so wrong in many areas, but thought I was so right. Girls, have you ever been there?

I thanked God for His Word and prayed for the Holy Spirit to teach me. Thinking about my pain and hurt made me realize that my responses were neither always correct nor were they Biblical. How could that be? I was always a woman of integrity as far as forgiving the people who hurt me. Certainly, this was not my problem. Yet my new friends taught me a deeper truth.

Now for the next several years we attended special classes. We had a personal prayer ministry where I could actually tell my story, and they empathized with me. Then the hammer was lowered ever so gently. I began to pray prayers that were ready made for the occasion, "Father, please forgive me for my response to this sin and the way it affected me." Thanks to John and Barbara Briggs, and dear Gerry and Gladys Funk.

In all my years in the church and in a full time ministry, never before had I heard these words. I was set free as I began to ask the Lord to forgive me for my response. How simple, but how freeing! I took this knowledge home with me and began to apply it to areas in my life untouched by the healing presence of God. The Scripture in Luke 4:18 came alive as I could feel strongholds crumbling inside of me. I now reacted differently to situations which before would paralyze me. God was doing a healing work in my life.

If this chapter brings you any pain or discomfort, perhaps the Lord wants to draw attention to your wounds. Your symptoms may be bitterness, fear, or lack of trust. Maybe you have suffered from the hands of the saints. While it seems, and probably is, unfair we must remember that no matter whom the devil has duped into being the vessel willing to bring destruction to a pastoral family, it is ultimately the work of the devil. *"For we wrestle not against flesh and blood, but against principalities, against powers, against the rulers of the darkness of this world, against spiritual wickedness in high places"* (Ephesians 6: 12 KJV) Let's put the blame where it belongs. God did not do this to teach you a lesson; the devil did this to destroy you.

Girls, Would You Pray This Prayer with Me?

Father God, I have been hurt by the betrayal, the lies, the rejection of _________ (name the church, the board members, the presbyter board who agreed with them, the members who came against you.) They have wounded my soul to a point where I do not know if I can continue to pastor or preach or support my husband. What they did was unfair and wrong. But, I am willing to forgive them, just as you forgave me, Lord. I forgive _____________who has allowed the devil to use them to try and destroy me and my family. I forgive them for harming my family. The people did not hide their disrespect for their Dad and said things in front of the children that caused them to be fearful and bitter. I forgive them for hurting my husband and causing him sleepless nights and ill health. I forgive them for the snubbing me, for pretending or not caring I was close to them and how they continued with the conversation that bashed my family and my husband's or mine ability to pastor. I forgive them for bringing reproach to the church and to Jesus Christ.

Please forgive me for the ways I have responded to _________, out of my hurt and pain. I was wrong for the way I have responded. I was wrong for the words I spoke and the actions I took against them. I release them from any unforgiveness, punishment or from any debt they owe me. Please help me to love your people again. Amen.

Chapter 5

He's Discouraged

Fact:

- 1,500 pastors leave the ministry each month due to moral failure, sprirtual burnout, or contention in their church[23]

It's Monday!

Girls, we all know what this means: Sunday is over and some say "Thank God!" It has been a long week. Now Monday is here, and we have to watch our husbands go through the occasional (or all too frequent times) bout of being discouraged. The old pastoral syndrome, the "Monday Blues," he critically looks over yesterday, picking apart the service, the sermon, the response, the attendance, and the offering.

This can be very disheartening to our spouse, not to mention our family. He wants his church to be successful and grow. Just when he thinks it will, the snow storms begin, the summer slump comes, graduations commence, the Packer season arrives, you name it. The people have other things to do that Sunday. The pastor is embarrassed; he had more visitors than he had elders! Sometimes the man's ego and identity become entwined in his church. If church does not go well, he may place all the blame and guilt on himself. He may blame other people for the perceived failure. He may be dealing with large amounts of rejection, discouragement, and anger.

Fear may grip his heart to imagine what could happen when the people do not show up. He takes his frustration out on his wife and family

I know one thing: he will logically try to work at this until he reaches a sort of understanding. This can be a long process; he is not just discouraged, now he is trying to pull you into the web of "where are all the people?" This can be problematic.

Most pastors do not sleep well on Saturday night. Try as they might, many are rehearsing the sermon in their mind, reviewing their notes and praying. Since I also preach, I know Saturday nights may not be pleasant for the man, especially if he does not "fly by the seat of his pants" when delivering the message of the hour.

Think of it this way, girls: we are planning a party. Everything is set. The invitations were sent and many said, "I'll see you on Sunday." You are excited that this party will be a great time, but now they start calling you with all types of flimsy excuses:

- Something mysteriously came up but no information is offered.
- The kids are sick, which is understandable.
- Visitors unexpectedly showed up.
- Busy.
- Forgot.
- Friends invited me to their party.
- Sports involvement became the priority.
- "I just feel like staying home. I have been gone all week."
- And the worse of all: "I did not feel led."

Certainly, it seems reasonable why the mom with the sick baby could not make it because she was up all night. However, when they ignore simple good manners to call and say in advance they will not make it but do not come, and you have prepared for them something special, it hurts and offends. Now think of your husband's feelings. He is hurt. It does not matter how capable he is or how filled with charisma he is. He still can be hurt and offended, which can lead to great disappointments and discouragement.

Some may read this and think that man should not depend on the response of other men, but of God. That can be judgmental, since a shepherd's heart is about the people. Yes, I know you "do not count the people," but at the same time, the position God hopefully gave you to pastor and care for the people do require Sheep!

I have heard many clichés over the years from people who do not understand the heart of a pastor. That is why you do not leave your circles of spiritual friends for counsel. Others may not have a clue as to what you may be feeling, and the last thing you need is someone making light of what you are going through. The Lord is giving pastors' abilities and training to counsel other pastors and to meet the need of an ever-growing population of discouraged ministers.

Survey:

- 80% of pastors and 84% of pastors' wives feel unqualified and discouraged in their role as pastors.[24]

Not all Monday's feel this way. I do not want to paint a bleak picture or be melodramatic, but girls, when this does happen it is helpful if we could hear them out one more time. Then after they say whatever it is, we must try to get them into a better frame of mind. I know this can be difficult especially if he worked extra hard on his message and seemed more optimistic than usual. At that point, we need to treat them with TLC. The world would say not to be co-dependent, but I believe we are one. When one of you hurts, the other feels the pain.

Just Let the Man Talk!

We have the ability to encourage him when he is down. God Bless the Woman of God for extending her heart to the husband/pastor, as he does not have a large circle of friends or peers to talk to at times. His ego and his identity are at stake here. He is vulnerable and needs to talk, but remember*: he does not want a lecture from his wife*. Ouch! I needed to say that! As with any husband, they do not expect us to fix it or launch another lecture. They want us to listen, but not with an answer waiting or a criticism of what he could have done better.

Girls, I know we have probably all made the same mistake of telling him how to do it better or your way. This is not time for that; do not close him off by shutting him down with your criticisms and harsh looks. I think of Job's wife and the infamous words she spoke when Job troubles began: "Curse God and die." Mrs. Job, that was a little much, and quite over the top! (Job 2:9-10 KJV)

I know you were in the Sunday Service as well, and you saw the despondency, the lack of participation, or the lack of people. Where were all the people? We all process this differently. This is the time to stay strong. Remember, that you will have your moments when you need to lean on your husband/pastor, but right now, he needs you to lean on.

It is his day off and he may have not even prayed yet. Maybe he won't for the whole day. Maybe he is mad or sad and only wants to talk. Let him! Someday you will want him to share, and he will not because of you always rushing to the rescue. You have not been allowing him to express himself, which has shut him down too often. It is all right to vent to his wife, so let him get it out of his system. It may scare you, but let the man be real instead of having to spare your feelings because he is frightening you. You'll get over it, and so will he.

Now, since we know the man needs to talk and vent, just give him a chance to pray later. There are things he may like to do as an outlet for his pent-up anger or depression. If he likes to golf, encourage him spend a certain part of the day with his friends to golf. Some can lose themselves in caring for the lawn or repairing the house. He may not even talk until he has spent time doing what he loves to do. (Some men push this to the limit!)

I'm Concerned

The matter I become concerned about is not his chosen 'release' activity, but when this consumes more time than the Lord or the family. Something is wrong. Who will confront him? The board of elders? Most will not even know, but hopefully you as the wife will have the ability to get through to him. He cannot continue to hide behind a golf cart or in the middle of the lake fishing. He needs to have a little discussion with Jesus to tell him his troubles. This is acceptable on Monday, when the excuse is "I am disappointed about Sunday." But now this is Tuesday or Wednesday, and it is a workday!

Remember the old joke told at nearly all pastoral conferences? "Get up and go to church. No, yes, you get to church. No, I do not want to go! You have to, you're the preacher!" That gives us a chuckle, but there are times he does not want to see the church doors for a long time. He has had enough and just needs to take a rest.

You know what I mean girls, when this has gone on longer than it should. It is time to confront him before someone else does. He is safe with you, so keep it that way. Do not let anyone know except for his faithful pastoral friends who can help, encourage, pray, and give him godly counsel.

This is a time to make him aware of his escape mechanism and help him get back on course. Some people are mistaken if they think the man is so strong that they can manage everything they are feeling by themselves. We have made men into an egotistical loners, fooled into thinking that they are tough and do not need anyone. That is by far the worst lie ever told; they are lonely and need companionship as well.

The Bible says we need to adapt ourselves to our own husbands. This is a true statement, and women, we need to notice this and start doing what the Bible teaches us about our husbands. Too much of the world has crept into the church, to the extent that we put "me" first, thinking we should pursue our own happiness and fulfillment. We are to minister to our husbands especially when we see trouble on the horizon in his personal life and ministry. We have cut ourselves off from the true plan of God when we have attitudes like the world.

> *In like manner you married women, be submissive to your own husbands – subordinate yourselves as being secondary to and dependent on them, and adapt yourselves to them. So that even if any do not obey the Word (of God), they may be won over not by discussion but by the (godly) lives of their wives, When they observe the pure and modest way in which you conduct yourselves together with your reverence (for*

> *your husband. That is, you are to feel for him all that reverence includes) to honor, esteem (appreciate, prize), and (in the human sense) adore him; (and adore means) to admire, praise, be devoted to, deeply love and enjoy (your husband).* (1 Peter 3:1-2, AMP)

What Is She Thinking?

I know some of you are thinking, "What is she thinking?" Just the Word, girls. We need to be our husband's biggest fan, whether he wins or loses the "Monday Blues." Keep strong, keep watchful, and keep vigilant. Eventually, something may cause you discouragement and you lose heart, and he can be there for you. This heart attitude can bring a couple closer together if you both understand that what the enemy of our soul means for evil, God can turn it for good. It can be a great victory when a husband and wife team set the enemy to flight. The Scripture talks about the three-fold cord that is not easily broken: you, your husband, and the Holy Ghost. What a team! (Ec. 4:12 KJV)

Discouragement comes to all of us, but we are not to stay there. Work toward resolution. Do not let it cripple you since it can do so if you yield to it. Go back to work, pray clear through, and immerse yourself in the Word of God to renew your mind DAILY.

Where is the Happy Medium?

I am concerned for husbands/pastors who suffer from discouragement and discover their wife may be insensitive to the problem since it has lasted so long. She feels indifferent to the man of God, since she is done trying to get them out of the Monday Blues Syndrome that has lasted far too long. "He's a big boy, and he can take care of himself," or "He'll get over it," or "I am done trying," are all statements that may be plaguing her mind.

If you women of God are letting statements like this come out of your mouth, please realize they are literally coming out of your heart. It seems to me that you have a problem as well, and it is called bitterness. When you carry this type of bitterness, the Word says that you defile many. You are also defiling your husband! He is having a hard time overcoming this depression or discouragement and some of the problem is the way you treat him. I know I am being hard on you, but someone has to let you know as well that this is sin. You are in direct disobedience to the Word of God, *"Looking diligently lest any man fail of the grace of Go*d*; lest any root of bitterness springing up trouble you, and thereby many be defiled;"* (Hebrews 12:15 KJV) I love how the Amplified Bible makes it very plain: *"Exercise foresight and be on the watch to look (after one another), to see that no one falls back from and fails to secure God's grace (His unmerited favor and spiritual blessing), in order that no root of resentment (rancor, bitterness, or hatred) shoot forth and cause trouble and bitter torment, and the many become contaminated and defile by it."*

To look further into the Scriptures, we understand Hebrews was talking about Esau; he sold his birthright for a bowl of soup! Is it far too easy to think we are drowning and give up, that we cannot be helped or rescued from the sinking ship of life or ministry?

How can we help you to get out of this cycle? It can eventually disqualify you from being pastors. Do you realize that whatever is preached or projected from the pulpit eventually trickles down to the congregation? If you do not keep your relationship pure and clean with your husband, and he goes into the pulpit with discouragement, sin, and despondency, it will affect the people. They usually do not catch on right away, but eventually the people will start questioning your message, your fervency, your call, your counsel, and it begins to snowball. We can blame it on the people for a while, but then it will come back to you pastors. What is going on in your personal life? What is going on in your marriage?

Have you noticed that the people are not as excited about their personal walk with God, and it seems like church is now an obligation? Do you see that they are not contributing much excitement, interest, time/talents, or even money? What has happened? Where did it originate? Are they following the shepherds lead?

This may be hard for you, but issues do have a beginning or root. Yes, certainly some go back as far back as your parents but some issues concern the things you have done in the ministry. When was the last time you took a personal inventory of yourself? What would be the inventory's criteria? Check all those which pertain to you:

- Do you dread your Sunday morning service all week long?
- Do you wait until the last day or hour to prepare your sermon?
- Do you feel anxiety when you awake on Sunday?
- After a Sunday morning service, do you complain about it?
- After a Sunday morning service, do you become depressed or angry?
- After a Sunday morning service, do you thank God for what He did during the service?
- Are you excited to give the message God gave you for the people?
- Do you consider that God even speaks to you through His Word?
- Did you spend time in His Word each day of the week?
- Did you spend time in personal prayer?
- Did you spend adequate time in preparation for the sermon?
- Did you get your last sermons from TV or old sermons so you did not have to work so hard?
- Do you feel fire in your bones when you preach the Word of God?
- Do you even want to preach when attendance is low?
- Do you consider it an honor and privilege that you are called to preach the Gospel of Jesus Christ?
- Are you excited about what the Holy Spirit is doing among your people?
- Have you lost your joy?
- Have you lost your focus or cause of Christ?
- When was the last time you had an altar call for salvation in your church?
- Do you have many sleepless nights because you are concerned about the church?
- Do you have sleepless nights because of someone in your church causing division or creating factions?
- Are you afraid to confront people in your congregation, fearing that you would lose them?
- Are more people leaving your church than coming in?
- Is there anyone you need to forgive?

- Do you need to ask someone to forgive you?
- Are you comparing your congregation to someone else's sheepfold? Are you jealous?
- Is it getting easier to find fault than to give thanksgiving and praise for where God has placed you and the assignment He has given you?
- Have you isolated yourself from your peers who would be able to speak into your life and ministry if given the opportunity? Do you return calls or do you screen all calls that do not pertain to your exclusive ministry?
- Are you comparing yourself to what you think or what others think is a successful Pastor?
- When was the last time you made a special trip to an altar to pray and repent?

I take responsibility along with my husband. I am yoked with him and have seen, heard, and felt many of the things I have asked. It is not good to point a finger at the congregation and blame them for where we are spiritually. Yes, something they said or did may have hurt us, but we have taught forgiveness, and now therefore forgive and move on. A survey taken of some pastor's wives surprisingly revealed that some have never taken a consecutive two-week vacation in their entire pastoral career. Among their listed reasons:

- Fear that the church will like the substitute pastor better.
- No money.
- The pastor's have to work a secular job and cannot take any time off since they have sacrificed all their vacation time for church activities
- They do not feel the need to rest or to be away from the toil of the ministry. You have never taken the time to rest.
- They do not trust the people to take over for them

Don't Let Him Drift Away

Pastors' wives, I am concerned for your relationship with your husband and for your husband himself. There are too many stories where the husband ended up having an affair with someone in the church, or was caught at an X-rated movie house, or with porn, or with another woman, man or child! The list goes on and on these days, and I do not want to put a scare into you. However, we do have a responsibility to our husbands to minister to their needs. Most women immediately think of sexual needs, and of course, that is part of it. Let's talk about their need to have you around and understand what they are going through. I know at times you will have plans made, and he would not want to keep you from going out shopping and having lunch with the girls. Yet we should have awareness to realize that we need to stick close to home for his sake, and to let him know that there is always another day for shopping with the girls. This day belongs to him.

Try to Get Out of Dodge

Please girls, begin to pray for your husband. He has a call of God, and it weighs heavily on him, either by not doing the will of God or just the task at hand. There are times in the middle of the night that I will lay hands on my husband and pray for him, that his mind be fresh, his body healed, and that he would have the message that God wants him to speak, flow, and develop. I pray that all hurts are washed away by the cleansing stream of the Word of God. I pray that whatever is bothering him the Lord would take control and bring him through the situation. The good thing too is that he prays for me in the same fashion.

When you know your husband is struggling with something, ask him if you could pray for him. So much talk and very little prayer! Pray until you get a "word of the Lord" for him, as he is waiting to hear. To get some type of encouragement, let the gifts flow in you for your husband.

Back in the 1980's, Dennis and I went on a vacation to see the wonders of the Rocky Mountains. This alone can be healing therapy. We decided to find a church to attend on Sunday. The pastor seemed to be under some kind of pressure. He began talking, not preaching or teaching. He talked beyond the appropriate time of a normal service. To our surprise, all of a sudden, he became angry, stomped off the platform and walked out the side door. No dismissal, no God bless you, he was gone! We were dumbfounded to say the least.

Even as pastors, we did not know what to make of it: do we get up and consider ourselves dismissed, or will he come back in for another round?

We felt so sorry for the man and for the congregation. We could only pray for him as we traveled down the mountain, thanking God, and realize that we did not have it so bad after all. We learned a good lesson that day; the sheep do not have to be entangled in the discouragements of the pastors. You have an ability to get up and preach the Word of God. You do not have to take this out on the sheep. Have your own conference with the Lord before the service so that you can present the sweet spirit of the Lord.

Often times we misrepresent Father God when we allow ourselves to act like that. If we do not have control over our emotions, we should take a rest before someone in the congregation feels like you need to take a long rest.

I have found if the trusted elders and the advisory board know some of our trials, they will "watch out" for us and pray for us to come through the test. Many times, we do not allow anyone to know our feelings. We keep at arm's length the ones God has given us to come along side of us to help. They are chosen for their mature spiritual nature and insight, and it would be their honor and privilege to uphold us if we would be honest with them. You could even have one or two come into your office and pray so that you would be able to minister and focus on what the Lord has instructed you to give the people.

I have a dear friend who knows how nervous I become when I occasionally preach. She seeks me out, puts her arms around me, and prays a blessing over me. The warmth of the Holy Spirit that resides in her blesses me and my nerves are settled. Thanks, Kay.

Many times my husband has been discouraged, and I asked him how could he preach when feeling so badly. The secret is he can separate what he is going through from his responsibilities at the given time. He leans into the anointing of the Lord and prepares himself in the Holy Word.

I am an "occasional" preacher and thank God I am, as I have not learned what my husband knows. He has protected me several times when it was my turn to preach and the enemy ambushed me. My feelings were hurt, and I was not sure of my response. I am comforted in knowing that even in the midnight hour he can take over for me, since I would not want to hurt the sheep by my emotional response.

Many times pastors will use the pulpit as an opportunity to punish the sheep, a sort of punching bag, which is not what God intended. Women, if you are having an emotional time, stay out of the pulpit if you cannot trust your emotions and if you cannot lean into the anointing to preach or teach. I think of that scripture about how a man is stronger than the woman is and he needs to consider us to the place he wants to protect us. In addition, we bare one another's weaknesses, and two are better than one if one falls down the other can help him up. (I Peter 3:7; Ec. 4:9-12 AMP.)

I am a firm believer that we are responsible for our actions. When we are enduring the dreaded PMS (Pretty Mean Sister), we need to back away from the duties where we may actually hurt people by our words and actions. If you are going through PMS, get to a medical doctor or nutritionist who can help you. Do not stay in this state of being angry and saying whatever you please, it is not becoming the Woman of God. We do not have a license to say whatever wants to come out of our mouth.

Please, Pray This Prayer with Me

Dear Lord God,

My husband and I are in the midst of a storm, and it looks like we are about to sink in this boat called the church. I believe you called my husband to preach the gospel and pastor this church. Thank you for the Call. Thank you that you knew we could do it for you.

Lord, your Word says that we need to humble and submit ourselves to you and resist the devil. We humbly come before you this day to say we have been wrong; we have not done everything according to your Word and your plan, and we repent of this. We want to love the people you have entrusted in our care. Give us your agape love, so we can do that.

We have been operating out of our own love and strength, and it is not working. Please forgive us for the things we thought, for the words spoken out of our mouth. Forgive us for agreeing with what is contrary to your Word. Lord, we forgive the people who have hurt us. Please forgive us for our response to them, for every time we became angry, every time we isolated ourselves and pull away from the sheep. Please forgive us for lying and not speaking truth to the sheep when they hurt us. We packed it away in our chest of hurts and grudges. We could not trust their response or our own. Forgive us for not being the strong and loving leaders you wanted us to be.

Now we speak to despair, to anger, to depression and discouragement: we renounce you and all your tactics. We break agreement with you and how you make us feel. We resist you, devil, and you must flee from us. You will not influence our life. We proclaim that we are free from the bondage of sin and distress. Thank you Jesus for you have set us free by your power, love, and Word. We now purpose in our heart to renew our mind daily by the Word of God and not allow the enemy to have any ground. Thank you Jesus for your great love you have for us. Thank you for making us faithful pastors to your people. We love your people. Let us show it.

In Jesus' name, Amen

Chapter 6

What to Do When They Say Good Bye

Girls, to me one of the most difficult times we face is when the people keep leaving through the revolving door. As both a pastor's wife and a pastor, I try to look at this from the experiences we have had in the ministry so you can understand and help your husband deal with this continual issue. Some will cause you to grieve, while others will make you wonder what you did now. Perhaps some may even have you leaping for joy when they leave. See if you identify with any of these.

Empty Clouds

In my experience when someone comes, joins your fellowship, and says the words, "Oh Pastor, you are the greatest shepherd of God's flock that I have ever known. You are such an anointed preacher and teacher," and they begin to list all of your qualities within the first or second visit to your church, I start waiting for the other shoe to drop. This type of person is searching for something almost like the pot of gold at the end of the rainbow. They cannot settle down long enough to mature, since they think they are going to miss out on something at the church down the road.

We all experience this type from time to time. At first you are disappointed that they will not stay with you. They have all the potential to be a great asset to the church, but they are looking for something better than what you can offer. Now when I see these

Empty Clouds, I do not get excited since I know that they are just empty clouds moving across the open sky. They are not willing to hear. I still try to offer a bit of wisdom to them, because if they have a teachable spirit they will listen. My advice is usually that they need to find a church and settle down, since the Holy Spirit is grieved about them moving around and not taking the instruction of a pastoral staff. It is hard to pin them down on some of the issues in their life that need to be changed. Change usually comes from a person trusting a pastor/shepherd enough to allow them speak into their life. This will not happen if they refuse to stay put long enough for someone to correctly teach them, since they are used to eating on the run. Empty Clouds prefer smorgasbords.

One of the various responsibilities of the shepherd is the ability to examine the sheep and to determine if they carry deadly parasites that would harm themselves or others. There may be bruising or some broken bones that need to be set. They may be skittish and unable to rest beside the still waters. They need much care but refuse to accept it by running away from those who can help them the most. Ps. 23; *... thou anointest my head with oil*; Ps. 91; 3. *Surely, he shall deliver thee from the snare of the fowler, and from the noisome pestilence.* (KJV)

I am not so concerned about them popping in and out of the church. Their day will come when the Holy Spirit will deal with them. If they continually refuse to be pastored and they allow this lack of discipline in their lives, they will disqualify themselves from the great plans the Lord actually has for them.

God Told Us We Have to Go

More than once, if people have decided to leave the church, they give us a good meal to wash down the bitterness of the words, "God told us we have to go." I did not know if I should be mad at God for again telling them to go, or angry and disappointed at the people. How do you argue with the people when they say "God said?"

One of the most difficult challenges we face as pastors is when an influential member leaves. It is more than likely that they will have others follow after them. The others may think it is only right that they follow them, since in some way they may have been mentoring them and they may have had intimate fellowship with one another. I truly believe there is a right and a wrong way to leave the church. It should be after they have discussed the situation and prayed with the pastors and elders, so that they try to look for a solution from the Word of God and pray to find His perfect will. This is a principle that is not used as much as it should be to resolve the kind of issues that cause people to leave the church prematurely or correct the matters that would cause others to leave.

I am amazed how we are caught off guard when confronted with people leaving. We would benefit to have a paper that we have prepared with all the scriptures references concerning leaving a church, so we can actually give them out when people have a question. It is much better to have evidence from the Bible, so that they do not think this is just your opinion or judgment.

Who Is Asking For The Next Dance?

Girls, another predicament we face as pastors is the fact that other ministers do not see anything wrong with "courting" your people. If you do not have every function available to the people, some sheep start wandering! You would think that there would be rules of conduct between churches, but there is not. It is like the church with the most programs win! It is hard to think that there is much loyalty in the body of Christ today. At times, we are the ones with the great new program and people come. They may be dissatisfied with their pastors and think that our church is where they want to be. If they give us time to help them make the decision, we try to ask them first "Have you talked to your pastors about this? Can we work out a solution? Have you attempted to forgive the pastor or leaders?" We have people that are elusive. They love to come for the praise and worship and the good bible teaching, but they will come late and leave before anyone has a chance to ask them any questions or get to know them.

Sometimes, another pastor is wooing them, and it looks as if the grass is greener and more fruitful in his pasture. Promises are made, positions are offered, such as the prize status of worship leader, not to mention head intercessor or the coveted office of an elder. (This usually has to do with the person's desire for power and control.

They may feel the pastor does not appreciate or see all their abilities and anointing.)

My questions to you, dear pastor who builds his church with another shepherd's sheep, would be:

- Do you not think the previous pastor would have promoted them?
- Did you ever stop to think that this talented or gifted person must have some flaw that has disqualified them from ministry at this time?
- Did you ever think to check with the previous pastor as to the "story" they gave about why they were not in leadership?
- How will you set them down and discipline them? How will you disappoint them after you have promised them so much? What will happen if they revert back into old degenerative ways of living?
- Will you be the next victim of this man or woman who will not allow anyone to speak correction into his or her life?
- Will you ignore the real problem of the sin they have in their life, in order to use them to promote your church? Are you concerned that you are not promoting Christ and Him crucified by agreeing with their "pet sin?"
- Do you understand the Scripture: *A little leaven leavens the whole lump?*(I Cor. 5:6-8 KJV)
- Do you just think that the previous pastor did not "understand" the person who left?

Dennis and I spent six months living on a farm where they raised sheep. It was interesting to watch the lead sheep leap over nothing, and then all the other little sheep would leap over the same nothing! A different issue that hurts is that the first family may have reasons to leave but because many sheep follow the lead sheep, they just go away without ever taking counsel to see if this is a good move for them as well. This causes the pastor much hurt knowing that the sheep is not beckoning to his call, but ignoring the shepherd's voice to follow another.

I read that when the shepherds would come to a sheepfold, they would put all the sheep into one area. Then when it was time to leave, the shepherd would open the gate and begin to call his sheep. Even though there could be many sheep all sharing this same resting place, when the shepherd began his call, "come, come, little ones," the sheep would know their master's voice and move through the crowd to follow the shepherd to his pasture. (John 10:27 KJV) "*My sheep hear my voice, and I know them, and they follow me*"[25]

Please! I Have Heard This Song Before. . .

This can be such a soulful hurt in the lives of a pastor and his family. It does not matter how many sheep you pastor, when the dreadful words come you want to run, fight, or just say "Go! I do not want to hear this same song and dance that I have heard so many times before." Now for some of you who do not want to admit that this hurts, I can tell you that it does, at least in the beginning. But you have grown callous to the effects. You have found ways to protect yourself from the feelings of abandonment or rejection. You may be beyond feeling since it has happened more than once, and you have grown accustomed to how you deal with it. Beware, though, because anger, depression, or an 'I do not care' attitude can lead to bitterness.

Would it make a difference to you if I said this happens to all pastors and churches? Yes, you probably have been available to your pastor friends that are going through the pains of people leaving their church, trying your best to comfort them and reassure them that they are still called to preach. It happens, but how do you get rid of the feeling of being rejected yet another time? First, we have to face the fact that people will leave. Secondly, we need to be able to confront them with a concerned shepherd's heart. This can be difficult if we do not know how to confront properly.

Let us look at several scenarios and try to find ways to make a difference, I know when I was young in the ministry this would be devastating to me. I would cry, mourn, and feel like it was my fault. I would feel like God did not love me, and I was a failure since the people would not stay with me. Therefore, I began to explore my feelings, read, and seek help for what I was going through. This proved to be one of the best things I have ever done.

Now when people leave, I find that I react differently. Maybe this will help you also. Instead of ignoring the problem, face it. If they give you an opportunity to visit with you, find out why they want to leave. We would ask a few questions:

- What were the instructions "God Said to You"?
- How did you come to this decision?
- You have taken out membership with this church, and now you change your mind? Why?
- You said, "God told me to come to the church." When did God change His mind? What changed your mind?
- Have you fulfilled the promises you made the pastors? Have you done the work**?**
- Has anyone hurt or rejected you in this church that you would leave? Can we work this out?

Ohhh, Pastor Sandy! God Said. . . .

Many times facing this rejection leads to more rejection. You can feel dejected due to the words you heard these people speak about you, the church or your family. For some strange reason, girls, we take this very personally.

I remember one time a man came to me in the narthex. He was so religiously spiritual that I knew this was going to be something I did not want to hear. Nevertheless, I listened in spite of what I was sensing was going to be the "God Said" rejection. "Oh… Pastor Sandy! God is calling me to do a great work." I said, "And what would that be?" He continued, "He is calling me to go be with this new pastor coming into town. Pray for me." I was not a bit happy, since he just came out of our new membership class! I said to the man, "Let me understand this, you just came from membership class where you have told the leader you believe God has sent you to this church, and now you are going because now God is sending you somewhere else? Has God become double-minded that He cannot make up His mind where you should go?" Needless to say, the man had already made up his mind and there was no reasoning with him.

He was very ignorant of protocol. This can be so disheartening to a pastor and wife. Sometimes we sit and rack our brains trying to figure out how to keep people. It is a real dilemma for most pastors and families not to become cynical and to keep a sweet spirit.

This Really Hurts

One of the worst ways people leave your church is through their own backsliding. It is hard to see them go. For goodness sakes, do everything in your ability as spiritual leaders to redeem them! It makes it difficult when they neither want God, nor do they want any advice from the leaders. This is so sad to see this happen and then realize that they made the decision. It is as if they divorced you as pastors, and now they do not feel like they need to be under a covering to lead them back on the right path.

It is about time that we let people know how much it has damaged them over the years. Yes, I know this is about more than just the feelings of the pastor's wife. But I have visited churches where the wounded, worn out pastor's wife goes through the motions mechanically of being a dutiful pastor's wife. Inside, she is hurting. She does what has to be done, but there is no joy or sense of accomplishment.

You now know that I have been a pastor's wife and pastor for over 31 years, and I have felt like you do. However, I know through the healing touch of Jesus, we can be made whole and restored to new vitality and hope. One of the things that helped me was getting free from the fear of man. I was so afraid that I would either say or do something that would cause another to leave. I would second guess myself and assume I did wrong. I would rehearse the whole six months until I would finally realize it was not about me. I have to be obedient to the Lord and His Word, and when I do this, not all will like me, agree with me, or stay with me. As long as I have my heart right before God and people, the Lord will take care of the rest. I have asked the Lord to search my heart to see if there would be any wicked way in this pastor/pastor's wife, realizing that at times I am so wrong and need to repent to God and the people. When I humble myself and do this, I am in His will. It may not bring back the person or keep anyone from leaving, but my heart is clean. I know at times harsh judgmental words can be spoken, but the Lord wants us to grow up as well as the people. He wants us to cultivate the fruit of the Spirit in us and give us a new response. “Let the words of my mouth and the meditation of my heart be acceptable unto you oh Lord.” (Ps. 19:14 KJV)

It is disappointing when you realize just how many think they can say anything they want to you as if you are their slave. We are to treat them as we would treat a loved one because that is what they are. People are always watching and waiting for the response of the pastor’s wife. They expect something honorable from us, and we should be able to give it. I know we are human and we make mistakes as well as the people, but the difference we are to show is the example of admitting when we make a mistake and asking forgiveness. When we can be humble ourselves, it teaches the people to humble themselves. We are the shepherd, and they will follow our lead. When we are transparent and first in line to repent, to ask forgiveness, reconcile, we lead by example. This is not to say this is easy! It is a humbling experience to be the one wrong or the first to do it. We never know the response of the other, and we are wading it dark waters. God is concerned about our response! It has gotten us into many troubled waters! We do not like these waters of adversity we find ourselves in, but I know we can get out of them by asking the Lord for wisdom and help. I am not opposed to yelling “Help God, I am in dark waters by my own doing! Forgive me!”

When I finally could admit that I was an angry pastor’s wife, it was all ready too late for some. I had already hurt them with my anger, and I am very sorry for that. I realized that I would have to find the root of my problem and deal with that. I had to take a good look at myself. It was hard to do. No one wants to think that they are part of the problem. We need to think positive. If we are part of the problem, then we can also be part of the solution. I had to recognize my fear of rejection, and where it originated from. Here are some of the things I had to do to make the difference:

- Was this caused by my formative years growing up with my parents and siblings?
- Was it how people treated me in school?

- Was it how my husband put the church before his family?
- Was it my disappointment with God for letting this happens; after all He could control the situations?
- Is it due to the bitterness in my life, how I blamed God, my husband, and the church for where I am today?

You Do Not Have To Stay There

Whatever the cause, I know from experience that you do not have to stay there. The Lord is willing to take the heavy burden of sin and guilt off of you so you can be released to freely love the Lord God again, along with your husband and people of God. When he heals you of your bitterness, he replaces it with a new love for the people.

Girls, Let Us Pray:

Dear Father God,

I have seen where I have missed it; I have caused a root of bitterness to reside in my heart, defiling many. Please forgive me for the ways I have sinned by not trusting you or loving my husband. Forgive me for taking my anger out on the people and my family. I am wrong. I forgive all those who have hurt me over the years. Lord, I pray that you would heal my old wounds and the fresh ones. Take away this broken and wounded heart. Let me actually feel you healing me of this wound. I wait for you Father. Please forgive me for the ways I have responded to others which was not Christ-like. I have wounded people out of my own wounding. Please release me from this guilt and pain. They cannot meet my need only you can Lord, and I ask you to heal my heart. Thank you that when I pray you hear me and you will respond to a broken and contrite heart. Amen.

I AM OUT OF HERE!

There are many dynamics in play when people leave the church. It is hard to explain what all goes on in the hearts of people. As pastors and their wives, we do not want "most" people to leave our churches. It is hard to say good-bye and mean it when we speak a blessing over them, especially if their leaving brings great disappointment and hardship. This leads to the subject of "What do you do when people that have been with you for many years decide to leave?"

There are various reasons why people decide to leave the flock where they were born again

- There could be irreconcilable differences.
- The individual will start his or her own ministry work.
- They may not agree in the direction the church or the pastor is headed.
- The person is being transferred to another location.
- They may feel led to go help labor in another man's field.

At times, the pastor or wife will hurt or disappoint a faithful member of his congregation or ministry staff. The offender may only repair these times by humbling himself or herself and asks forgiveness. This is practical biblical principle, with freeing results for both parties.

Sometimes, the person will not accept your apology and cannot continue to work with you. The wound hurt deeply, and the offense is more than they can handle. Whatever it is, it is not fixable in their eyes. I find two areas which make this difficult to bear.

One-sided Reconciliation

Girls, have you ever been confronted with someone was angry or offended, after you had conflict with them? You took the "high road" and genuinely ask forgiveness. The person who is offended accepts the act of you humbling yourself, but they do not think there is anything that they need to ask forgiveness for as well. They are satisfied with your apology, but you feel like they had a part in the matter as well. It is all one-sided. You repented, but they did not feel the need. This can be like a slap in the face that will sting for awhile! Rest assured that you did your part; stay in love and peace.

I've Got Your Number!

Here's another one for you girls. This person now feels they cannot work with you any longer because of the offenses you have already repented over. They scrutinize you and wait for you to slip up again. It is difficult to always be on guard, lest we 'slip' and hurt somebody's feelings again. It's like walking on egg shells. It steals away our joy, we feel like failures in the relationship department, and it tries to keep us from speaking into other peoples lives that actually want to hear from us! Or on the other hand, it will make us very callous and bitter toward people where we do not care about their feelings at all. We become very authoritarian, making no excuse for ourselves.

Throughout the Bible, there are multiple references to forgiving. Forgiving also means forgetting. In this case, the Lord gives us grace to grow into what the Lord has planned for us.

Irreconcilable differences:

There are times that good men and women of God cannot and will not see eye to eye with the Pastor,

- They may not like how he conducts church services; he could be a radical as far as they are concerned.
- They may not like how someone was disciplined in the church.
- They may not like the music/worship style.
- They may not agree upon how the finances are used.

My question to them is: what brought you to this church and to this pastor? Did you once like the fiery preaching or his great faith? When did you realize that you did not like the way the church was going? Was it the time that you were not informed of a decision that was made and you were not in agreement? Did you think you could influence the man of God to change how he operates in his church? Was that presumptuous of you? Did you not realize that you were to submit to your spiritual leaders?

Pastor, why would you give in to what that one man or group of people wanted that gave them power that eventually persuade you his way? Did you not realize that sooner or later there would be a power struggle, and you would be misunderstood? Pastor, why did you ignore your wife when she warned you about that man, more than once? Why did you ignore the counsel of your friends when they also told you? Everyone could see it but you. What did he offer you that you would allow him to continue like an Absalom?

This is the time the pastor's wife comes to the forefront, as nasty as it may seem, with the words, "I told you so." So many times we see it coming from the horizon much sooner than our husbands. I believe God gives the pastor's wife a keen sense of knowing who will be a good friend to the pastor and who will try to use him to gain control. This can lead to deep bitterness between you and your husband. You are his helpmeet, but there are things that you are not allowed to speak into his life. Sometimes it is a warning. Let's face it, girls: at times he may think you are paranoid, and at times you actually may be! Especially if you have gone through this several times and have seen what it does to your husband, your family and the church. What can be frustrating is when a well-known preacher/evangelist comes and they see the issue the wife has discussed with him many times but to no avail. It is like the sun bursting through dark storm clouds for pastor, as long as someone else told him besides his wife.

This is a huge mistake in building a lasting relationship based on mutual trust and admiration. Girls, do yourselves a favor and pray more. It will pay big dividends in the end. Try to keep yourselves sweet. Ask the Lord for the right time to let your husband know about the problem you see. What seems to hinder many pastors' wives is that we always tell them every little thing we think is wrong, so when something big comes along, we blow it. Instead of our tongue being seasoned with grace, we become critical and skeptical about all the decisions he makes. He does not think he can win for losing. You already have him marked as a loser for an incident that happened years ago. You cannot forget it, so therefore you will see to it that he does not make that mistake again by bringing up his past failures in times of stress or when major decisions need to be made.

Pastors' wives, please forgive your husband for those mistakes that cost you your peace, your home, your friends, your church, your income. If you forgive him, then you can learn to trust him. He needs to be free to be the leader of the home and the church. If you forgive him, he may let you into his life. He may want your help and prayer when a decision needs to be made. He knows you are wise, but he cannot get through the bitterness you have created around his ability or inability to make wise decisions. We all grow up, we all have made mistakes, and we have learned from them. Trust and release him.

I Hear Loud Controlling Voices, But It's Not GOD!

I am so surprised by how many people want to have control over a church that is not theirs to have any authority in whatsoever. It does not matter whether you have 20 or 2,000 members. Someone wants to have a say, and he wants to have a louder voice than the voice of the pastor. The Bible says, *this should not be named among you*, but it is. You have done all you can to correct and teach the person, but he is now going behind your back for the vote. He is influencing men and women in the halls, the fellowship room, and the parking lot. He is not speaking on behalf of the pastors, but about them. He needs to have his authority taken away from him, and he needs to go. It is better for the man and his family to realize that there is no place of authority for him, and they need to leave. Keep your distance because I believe in the judgment of God. He is tired of the people disturbing the house of God by their selfish actions to usurp authority from the pastor and destroy the plan God has for the church. Sometimes it will stir the man of God to pray more or to get his house in order. But the other things that happen, the Bible clearly warns us, woe to them that cause the offense and division. (Matthew 18:7; 23:13-23 KJV)

I am not saying the pastor is necessarily right in all that he does, but he is accountable to God first. It is great to have an advisory board to help with duties in the church but greater to have the accountability of other pastors so that they can help you make the decisions that are hard for you. Consider them the "Veterans of Wars." They understand what could happen and can lead you in a righteous manner.

Parting is Such Sweet Sorrow….Not!

These people have been your friends. They have poured their life's blood and energy into your ministry. They have shared with you their dreams and plans for the church since they were working in the ministry with you as your team armor bearer, right hand men etc. The list goes on, but they are not with you now. Evidently something happened along their life's journey or in your relationship. Evidently they have grown too big for you in their own eyes, and they feel they have to move on and start their own work.

I believe this is a very disheartening problem for pastors. You think they are with you. You have spent quality time with them in the office and at dinner. Some even take vacations with the leaders. Then the dreaded day comes. They set up an appointment between the two couples, or all of those leaving at this time. The hearsay is true. You have expected something for a long time, but it did not seem to be in your grasp to put things back into working order. The pastor may have tried in his own way to fix it. Maybe he offered a gift, or a different position, where the person would feel more affirmed or valued, giving them a fresh start renewing his interest in the church. This may satisfy them for a short period, but eventually the stirring to be on his own, is there again, this time with a stronger force or demand on the pastor.

Oh, how many times we have gone through this in one form or another and wished that time would go back to where they had begun to feel the call of the ministry, to embrace the Pastors call as if it was their own, and stand behind the man and woman of God so they could fulfill their call. They came with their God-given talents and abilities and wanted to hook up with us. They had great ideas and wanted to be part of what God would do in the church.

They spoke words:

- "Pastor, all I want to do is be your armour-bearer."
- "Pastor, The LORD called me to be your assistant."
- "Pastor, I want to come and work for you. God told me to be your Joshua."
- "Hey Buddy, I've got your back side."

The very words that made you feel secure or exceptional and helped to convince you that God really did want to do something special in your ministry. The words these people spoke to you were proof that you were chosen for this ministry, or pastorate. The people were following you. They believed in your call, and you have felt that the anointing you have in your life is not just what your mom or your spouse thinks you have something of value to share. Now these same words haunt you. They ring in your ears as a laughing mockery. The devil knows just how to cause those uplifting words to torment you for a very long time. You rehearse what went wrong and wonder how you could have done or handled things differently. Then you spend much time trying to justify your actions, amid the turmoil, the accusation, the failure, the rejection, and the abandonment. Girls, I have seen this happen. We may not want to admit it hurts since it has happened before. We would rather take the stance of being unruffled, thinking, 'if people want to leave, just go, and don't let the door hit you on the way out.' They put up the invisible walls of defense and now the war begins. We join forces with our husband against the ones who abandoned us, trying to keep up the front that everything is all right without them.

Whose Idea Was This, Anyway?

Ouch! I have seen or handled this in several different ways. Some people fall into a deep depression. They feel like they have nothing left when their support system abandons them. What is left? Will they leave me too? The pastor's confidence level is at an all-time low. He may start questioning his own call. Has all of this been about my ego? Did my friends feed my ego? Did God really call me to preach and to pastor or was this my mothers idea? Just because my dad is a pastor that does not mean I had to be one too. Was I pressured out of the obligation that I had to follow suit because it's supposedly in my blood? Did friends of the family keep speaking over me that I was the next one to go into the ministry? Have I been afraid to seek God for myself, since I was the "Golden Child." After all, my parents are so and so. Talk about deep calling unto deep. This is the depths of depression and questioning the call of God. Was it real, did I hear it or did someone say to me, "you're called to preach?"

Girls, I know personally the feelings of being rejected and abandoned as a pastor's wife and pastor. It can be so devastating to us.

Usually, we take things differently than our husbands. A husband will shut down and will not want to talk about it until that horrible day that everything inside him bursts. However, we can talk about it forever. No need for my husband to say anything. I've thought of every negative circumstance possible! And he is the only one I can tell it to!

At times there is no peace. All sleep is gone and as such, you have not had good night's sleep in several days. Emotions are running at an all time high. It does not take much to cry or go into a depression. You may feel like you do not care about the obligations you have at the church. What is amazing is, whether we like it or not, it's business as usual at the church. You may not have the people in the same position as you had last week. Now you will have to add another job to the pastor's wife's endless duties. It is not pleasant to be in this position. You may not enjoy doing some of these duties, and you are not sure if you even know how to do the job. You resent the fact that the person that had this ministry before rudely walked out on you, or maybe they neglected it to the place where it now must be either scrapped or completely revamped. It makes you wonder how you could trust someone with a position of authority who did not consider the importance of their responsibility.

It Makes You Almost Paranoid

- "Did she sabotage this ministry so that she could punish me?"
- "Was she really feeling this badly? Why did I not check up on her and make her accountable for the mission we gave her?"
- "Why did I not see the warning signs that something was wrong?"
- "I thought she was my friend. I shared things with her, so now what do I do?"

The problem is our life does not stop. We have to continue to spread the love even when we feel very unlovable because of the actions of a few people.

Suddenly, the Dam Broke!

I will never forget the morning I put two grown men in a very uncomfortable position. One man, who was responsible for our Children's Church program, arrived early. He was a very nice man. He and his wife had the same kind of goals and dreams in the ministry. We had good times of fellowship and sharing. He could really get you laughing by some of the corny jokes he would tell. Then one day, while I was on my way to do the work of the ministry, I happened to go to the lower level of the church to check on my friends. I was confronted by this good-natured man who would not hurt a fly. He told me that he was leaving with his family. Our dreams of ministry were not their dreams any longer, and they would not help. Instead, they were leaving because he had better plans for himself. Well, with that said, my husband was just opening the church service! I could not disturb him with such matters before church because we always believe in protecting the time the Word of God is to be preached. Almost everything else can wait. Consequently, I carried it by myself, only as far as my car. I walked outside to the private area of the pastor's parking, got in my car and locked the doors. I began to wail. It was as if someone popped the cork on the champagne bottle of my emotions. I wailed so loud I could not stop. I do not even know if I had tears, but I wailed.

He Knew I was Unapproachable

Now a different man, who happened to come late for church, saw and heard me in my car wailing. He knew I was unapproachable, so he walked back and forth beside my car praying for me. While I wailed the man who popped the cork was watching helplessly from the entrance door, realizing that he picked an inappropriate time to harshly tell me they were leaving. I really had these two guys worried!

As a dutiful pastor's wife, I finally composed myself. I had nowhere to go, so I went into church, with red swollen eyes. The Children's Church teacher came to me to say he was sorry and that he would stay. I looked at him and said, "No, you do what you need to do. Do not let my tears keep you from what God wants for you."

I stood in the front row and began to worship God, since the song service was well under way. I will remember this time until I go home to be with the Lord. As I raised my eyes and hands toward heaven, I saw a mini-vision. I saw a hand with the little finger torn off, and then I saw cells rushing to it to make a new little finger (teaching gift). In my spirit, I heard these words, "My body is a living organism, and I will make it to grow again." I felt an inexplicable peace come upon me and I knew that God was with me and would help us through this time.

Now I would have to help my husband through this new hurt as well. I had just gone through the valley of the shadow of death of a great relationship, and now it was his turn to face and respond to the news. We grieved over the lost of great friends and co-workers.

This has caused me much heartache and soul searching. This is necessary at times, so girls, take the time to ask some vital questions;

- Do I take people for granted?
- What could I have done to help them or respond different?
- Do I appreciate the ministries that have been set in the church?
- Could I have prevented this?

I knew one thing for sure: I was going to have to forgive them. He did not try to hurt me. He was just trying to muster up enough courage to try to tell me his plans. Nevertheless, I was extremely hurt and rejected. Each time I was rejected (back in the day) I would react strongly. It was as if I could never heal long enough to feel better about myself and work on my response. We all have different ways of responding when we are hurt. Some get angry, over-eat food, take it out on other people, cry forever, or get lost in their work or sport. The list goes on; people may gossip or justifies their actions. Some punish themselves with negative self talk. What ever the case may be, we can wreak havoc on our emotions.

What a wonderful time when we finally let God into the emotion of it all, the betrayal, abandonment, rejection, anger, sadness. He actually said that he came to bind up the broken hearted and set the captives free. (Luke 4:18 KJV) That seems kind of odd that he came for us preachers. We are the ones to be there for the people so they know how God loves them. We always can have a good message for the people, but what about when I am so sad on account of the circumstances? I cannot talk about them, since whatever I say may be used against me in the "court" of the church. Those are cold, cruel words to a pastor's wife. Girls, they do not see how your husband cannot sleep at night or how he has no self-esteem left. He wonders what's going to happen to him when the board meets the next time, now that Mr. Money Bags has left the church.

The Saint was Hardly a Christian!

Over the years you learn more about God. He has been good to us. It took us awhile to understand just how good He is. Some of the things we have gone through have helped us grow strong and lean heavily into His arms. There is a place that even when the storm is raging, we can hide. I realized that it did not have much to do with "Spiritual Warfare." Yes, I have been praying for years and there is not much I have not personally done or taught in the church. There are not any surprises in prayer for me except this one thing. I would spend hours "fighting the warfare" with all types of prayer. One day I woke up to the fact that Jesus taught to love my neighbor as myself and to do good those who despitefully use me. I thought that could be for many people inside the church. I usually thought this of sinners and not saints, but as far as I was concerned, the saint was hardly Christian! As a result, I began to forgive and bless the people who had hurt me. It took awhile because I had a whole list! One by one, the list dwindled to nothing. I learned to keep this truth at the center of my personal life so that I did not get tangled up again with the resentments and bitterness that would result in sleepless nights. The older I get, the more I love to sleep all through the night. Remember the scripture "Do not let the sun go down on your wrath." There is a reason for the Scripture: it gives you better sleep!

Even "Good Things" Hurt

We do know that there will be times when some people have to go and start their own ministry. (Acts 6:1-7 KJV) This is supposed to be a good thing. They have learned all they will under your ministry. You have taught them well. Even if we do not want to see them leave, they will leave. They can leave with or without your blessing. Too many pastor's shoot themselves in the foot by not recognizing the pastoral call on someone else. The ideal situation is that as your own church grows, they can come on staff with you. This may not happen in their timetable, and they are anxious to be on their own. It could also be that the church cannot afford another full-time pastor. There is not much you can say to them, since it seems like they have been "waiting" a long time to them. You would like to warn them about all the things that could happen to them, but they think you are trying to discourage them. You are not. It's inevitable that they are going to take over a church or start one of their own.

Hopefully, they have learned what is proper, such as not starting a church just down the road from you, or taking on a church with bad history and no growth. Some churches cannot be fixed, especially if they have deeply rooted judgments and strife. The church could be steeped in false doctrine or financial distress.

If the young pastor will stay sweet and pray for an opportunity to pastor, the Lord will bring it to pass. I am more concerned for those who try to make their own way, only to get trapped in a church that is going nowhere. Another thing to consider is timing. At times the rest of the family is not as ready like the man may be, especially when they feel like they are being forced from all they know and love. This is not good; it should be a mutual agreement.

When it is time to leave, it should be done correctly. According to the book of Acts, the leaders prayed and fasted, then laid hands on the men to establish them in ministry. As they enter the pastoral call, there should be a celebration and prayers of blessings prayed over them. They will need their pastor soon. Do not cut off communication with them. Try to always have an open door policy. Some will go prematurely. You can warn them, but they will have to learn the rest for themselves.

It may be awhile before they realize that they are in trouble and lonely for their own pastoral care. Welcome them with open arms and have a listening ear toward them. They may have to boast for a while, but hopefully they will get real with you as to what they are experiencing. They are now ready to listen and take advice.

If you do not judge them for their zeal in wanting to get on with their own ministry call, they will want you to be their spiritual parents. They will come back into your lives much like grown children do; now realizing how wise you are. When they have tried all the programs, and they are not satisfied with church growth or the maturity of the saints, they will be looking for some spiritual advice and guidance.

Please Pray This Prayer With Me:

Father God, I am sad and mad. My life is filled with all sorts of disappointments. My heart is battered and bruised by the verbal beatings and the abandonment that I have felt over these years in ministry. I have not done everything right. I have been in the wrong many times. Please forgive me of my sins and the way I have responded to your people. I forgive ____________ for hurting me, for saying those words against me. I forgive them for their actions against me (slander, firing me, black balling me, cutting my salary, lying about my husband or children, believing lies about me, talking behind my back and dishonoring me, etc.)

I release them from being held prisoner by my own bitterness and unforgiveness. I release them, and I bless them. They are your children, and you are their Father. I take them out of the cage or jail that I have put them in, and I give them into your Fatherly hands. Please forgive me for the way I have responded to those that hurt me. I acknowledge that this was sin and does not become a Woman of God. Cleanse me from all unrighteousness. Please take the pain and wound from my soul, my mind, will, and emotions. Let me learn the lessons you want me to learn and cleanse me from every trap of the devil set up to destroy me.. Please forgive me for judging all people by the conduct of a few. Give me a heart to love your people through your Agape Love. Let the healing begin. Thank you Lord for your faithfulness and the Call of God I have on my life. Amen.

Chapter 7

I Am Not Your Mama or Your Ex-Wife!

The Dreaded Mother Issue

It can be very disheartening to a pastor's wife when, for no apparent reason, people treat you with dishonor. You have tried your best, but you just cannot get through to this person. They have distorted what you have said and read far more into your words or expressions than is really there. On most occasions, you may not be aware you have offended such a person. You may have been going about business as usual, but something in your mannerism triggered them to compare you with their mother. Suddenly you have it: The Dreaded Mother Issue

Usually, it is not your fault. Possibly she transferred to you whatever conflict she has with her mother. You may never know what triggered her. You share some of the same facial or body language expressions of the mother. Maybe you look or sound like her. Maybe you have a similar laugh or have the same type of humor as their mother has. Maybe it's as simple as wearing the same kind of perfume (Wounding). Sights, sounds and smells can trigger a person to recall a hurt caused by a parent. Perhaps your authority within the church to make decisions causes her to dislike you, since she did not agree with how their mother made decisions. (Rebellion and Contempt) She does not like her mother, and she does not like you.

(Unforgiveness toward mother) You reacted or answered like her mother did to her, with a harsh, hasty or exact answer. (Judgments toward mother) The person feels like you are too busy or important to ever have time for "getting to know the real you." (Abandonment and self pity issues) She feels that you have "favorites" in the church, and she is not one of them, therefore bringing rejection to the forefront. (Rejection)

Most likely, you will be suffering for this until the situation is set straight. Once you discover what the problem is, it is extremely important that you take steps to rectify any misunderstandings. It does not matter what set her off, but it does matter how you will handle the matter.

You're the Target

More than once this has taken me by surprise. I would be minding my own business, doing the work of the ministry, when it would happen. Some person, who never forgave her mother for something, now carries the same grudge against me. The majority of times, they are not even aware of the problem. When confronted with the problem, they may admit that, in some way, we do remind them of their mother. They realize that they have projected their unforgiveness, bitterness and fear towards the pastor's wife.

We as servants of God must take the high road and apologize for any misunderstanding. Remember Proverbs 15:1 says, *"A soft answer turns away wrath."* (KJV) I know we might feel the person needs to grow up and get over it. Yet, we also must remember that the value of the soul is greater than the value of being right. How much would it cost you if you didn't address the issue immediately? You do not want to have someone in your congregation who is a walled city, a very offended person who is not willing to work with you. Proverbs 18:19 says, *"A brother offended is harder to be won than a strong city; and their contentions are like the bars of a castle."* (KJV)

Just remember, girls, for each one you let go and ignore you are allowing them to talk among themselves and make unwanted judgments concerning you. You do not need this headache. In a very large church, this may not be a problem. In a small church where the pastors depend on most of their people to serve in one capacity or another, it would be a major hindrance to the growth and peace of the church. In forgiving and putting this offense aside, you may gain a friend; sometimes they just need more understanding and acceptance. This does not have to be an unpleasant task when they know the pastor's wife understands; it can be an unlimited gateway into ministering to the women of your church.

What I stated above is the ideal way to work out this conflict. Oh, if it was only foolproof! Some people take it a step further, voicing her dislike of the pastor's wife and sharing with others that the pastor's wife has offended her in some way. Suddenly it is very evident you have a greater problem on your hands. Now there's a faction, posse, or lynch mob watching every move the pastor's wife makes, collecting new evidence against her. This can easily escalate so that the pastor's wife may become the topic of almost every conversation they have. I am always amazed how people do not hide their looks of displeasure and can become downright rude, making snide remarks. Some may ignore her! This kind of treatment could make the strongest woman crumble.

This happens more than anyone would care to admit. The claws come out and the encounter begins, perhaps causing the pastor's wife to do a few things.

1) Withdrawal: She may come to church but have nothing to do with the people except for the pleasantries of surface conversation. She may come just when church starts and have an excuse to leave before the service is done. She will be fearful of most of the women and think that every woman in the church is against her, instead of just a small group. She will think that she does not have a friend in the church, and therefore will not reach out, but feel alone in the midst of a crowd.
2) Rejection and Depression: She suffers with hurt feelings, which results in wounds of the soul. There is nothing worse than when a group of people start picking on a lone pastor's wife. She is there to serve the people, and it can cause great distress to her and her family; it is a major cause of rejection and depression.

3) Bitterness: This will lead to bitterness of her soul if it is not taken care of properly. She will start a campaign of "if you really love me, you will candidate for a church somewhere she will be accepted."

Let the War Begin!

Now, not all pastor's wives go into isolation. Some cry out, *Let the war begin!* Those who have a great support system of elders and other leaders who respect her may retaliate with her own people. This has a nasty spirit, so beware that you do not fall into the trap the enemy has set for you. I have noticed that the enemy never goes far with his traps for it is too much work. The devil uses the old trap of contention between women, and it works every time! The cattiness of women must stop. When a pastor's wife or women in the church yield to such wrong sinful actions, pain and division are inevitable. No one wins, no matter how many words are spoken in your defense.

Even Paul mentions Philippians 4:2-3, "*I beseech Euodias, and beseech Syntyche, that they be of the same mind in the Lord. And I intreat thee also, true yokefellow, help those women which laboured with me in the gospel, with Clement also, and with other my fellow-labourers, whose names are in the book of life.*" (KJV)

Don't Let the Devil Knock You Off Track!

Many times, we can be on our way to success when we are thrown off the path of righteousness simply because we think we must be right. What we're not counting is the cost of what it will do to the plan of God, and this is pure selfishness. How disheartening that Paul actually used the word "intreat" which means "to beg." He wrote for all to see in the church that someone must step into this argument and take authority over it. Instead of nursing hurt feelings, we should be the ones to carry the Word of God in us so that we can make the first step in reconciliation. Now that would be a true woman of God!

From time to time, you may be able to minister to this angry person. If they need a mother figure in their life, they may allow you be the substitute. Sometimes they may cling to you, always wanting your approval. Both need to be corrected or they will suck the very life out of you. That is not what God wants. He wants us to be able to minister to all in the congregation, not just a few needy people. We were not meant to be a substitute for someone else, but we were meant to lead them into understanding of the Word of God that leads to repentance and reconciliation, so they can make peace with those that are estranged.

Use Your Major Weapon. . . Love

Over the years, I realized that people give away valuable information when they talk about their parents. Now, when I notice a person does not have a good relationship with her mother, I pay close attention to how she is treating me and with whom she is associating. I try to determine if she is trying to gather a faction around her. Some people would say ‘clique,’ but I use the word ‘faction’ since it can be evil and may plot against a leader. Paul did not mince words. He wanted people to beware of factions so they could be judged for what they were. Exercising that kind of authority will cause people to watch their hearts and mouths for any sort of disunity.

Nothing good that comes from disunity. Even if you did repent, the damage is done, and it is hard for the pastor's wife to move within that group of women to minister to them on any level. Many times the enemy wants to come in such a way that will cause such a wounding that it will stop the woman of God from doing anything else. You know if you stop the woman of God, you get to the man of God and his family.

Our weapons need to be weapons of love, such as "love thy neighbor as yourself" and "do good to those who despitefully use you." Many scriptures in the Bible speak of our conduct, which applies to leaders and laity alike. Too many pastors' wives have been very hurt in ministry and are too afraid to try again. We must remember to always act out of love and not fear.

Girls, I can hear you saying, "Yes, but how?" We must first take it to the Lord. As long as we fight this battle with our own strength, the enemy wins. Remember, our battle is not with flesh and blood, but with principalities and powers of darkness. If we have this understanding, we will spare others and ourselves much heartache and pain. We need to follow these easy guidelines:

1. Take it to the Lord in prayer, humble yourself, and seek peace.
2. Forgive the person for hurting you and for taking out her anger upon you.
3. Ask the Lord to forgive you for your response of fear, anger, revenge, gossip, etc. You name it and God will forgive you. "If we confess our sins, he is faithful and just to forgive us our sins, and to cleanse us from all unrighteousness." (I John 1:9 KJV)
4. Ask the Lord for a plan on how to approach her. "The Lord prepares a way before us." (Ps. 23:5 KJV)
5. Find a trusted prayer warrior in your church who can minister to her and bring her to repentance.
6. These women need a lot TLC, but not from you. Keep your boundaries.
7. Always be loving and kind toward her. Give no place to the devil.

Momma's Bad Boy!

Now women are not the only ones wreaking havoc for us girls in the church. Many men did not get along with their mothers and judged them harshly for their actions. This type of man has no respect for you as a leader. You can watch his "halo expressions" and see that the sooner he gets away from your presence, the better it is for him. He does not like it if you speak with authority. He does not like it if you voice a dissenting opinion. He does not like it if you are too loud or expressive. He may attempt to control you through his body language and his tone of voice. He may attempt to control the conversation by changing the subject so you do not get to say what needs to be said.[26]

If it is your turn to preach, this fellow will be up and out of his seat several times while constantly looking at his watch. You can find him out in the hall talking instead of respecting the woman of God. He will sit through the male pastor's message with ease. When the service is done, he will not let you know you did well. We are of no value to him.

Girls, this guy can make you miserable, especially if you do not know what is wrong. After all, they seem to like you if you are listening to their stories or are a visitor in their home. However, put you on a board or committee, and the battle begins. Usually, this is because they have not made peace with their mother, whether she is dead or alive.

Jesus Sets a New Standard

We do not live in the Old Testament times where women did not have much value in the Jewish community. Back then women were considered the same as a servant or dog, and they were owned as livestock were owned. This is one of the reasons that Jesus made it a point to stop and heal many women. Remember the woman with the issue of blood, unclean as she was, coming to Jesus? The law said she was not to go near anyone but to cry out, "Unclean, unclean," when people came close to her. She should have been punished when she crawled through the crowd to touch the hem of Jesus' garment. Jesus felt the virtue go out of Him and said, "Who touched me?"

We know the account. The woman had to confess what she had done, then face the consequences of the glare and punishment of men. She confessed with fear and trembling, not knowing what Jesus would do to her. An unclean woman touching Him was outrageous! Jesus did not rebuke her, but spoke kind and affirming words to her, saying, "Daughter, *thy faith hath made thee whole; go in peace, and be whole of thy plague*." Jesus also had to instruct her not to be afraid. I wonder if she was thinking of the aftermath when Jesus would go away. She would have to put up with what the men of the city thought about her desperate display, crawling through the crowd of mostly all men to receive something from God. (Matt. 9:20; Mark 5:25-34; Luke 8:43-48 KJV)

Jesus called her *daughter*, not slave or dog; He treated her with respect. He came to bind up the broken hearted and set the captives free. (Luke 4:18 KJV) Jesus wanted to a set new standard of accepting women with the same respect that men received. He is our example; we follow. Throughout the Gospels, He ministered to women with respect. Remember, He would stop a funeral procession just for a widow woman. He ministered to Peter's mother in law who was suffering from a high fever; He took time out of the busy schedules of people thronging Him and put everything aside to minister to one woman. (Matt. 8:14-15 KJV)

Let's turn next to the story about the Daughter of the Syrophoenician Woman Healed (Matt. 15:22-28 KJV). The woman was not even under any Hebrew covenant, but because she was persistent in asking and convincing Jesus that she would just take the crumbs off the floor from children's table, he healed her daughter. Jesus did not mind engaging women in conversation in a public place, even though the Pharisees of the day forbade it. The rabbis expressed contempt for women by teaching that they were not to be saluted or spoken to in the street, and they were not to be instructed in the law.

In John 8:1, when the Pharisees brought the woman caught in adultery, Jesus truly brought accusation to her accusers when He wrote in the sand, and they disappeared from Him, one by one. When addressing the sinner, He said, "Where are your accusers?" She told Him they were all gone, and Jesus said, "Go and sin no more." The law said to stone her, but He gave her back her life instead.

In John 4, we have the account of the woman at the well. Jesus said He had to go there. There, a woman of the streets had a divine appointment with the King of Kings, and brought revival among her people because Jesus took time to offer her the Living Water. He broke down walls of prejudice, racial barriers, and the stigma that a woman is not worth much, especially a prostitute. Jesus wanted His followers to realize that He came for all mankind. No matter what they were doing when He walked into their life, He treated them with the courtesy and compassion of His Father.

Jesus was not a womanizer. He wanted to change the state women were in due to the judgments of men. He wanted to bring them out of the darkness they dwelled in, and let them know that the Father loved them. I love it when Jesus first appeared to the women who followed His ministry and met His needs. The disciples were off by themselves, and the women stayed by the tomb. What a reward to be the first to see Jesus when He arose from the dead![27]

I am Not Your Ex-Wife!

Girls, you also need to watch out for those guys who may transfer their grievance of an ex-wife onto you. This may be a problem with men who are inside the church. These fellows usually carry such disrespect that they do not want to hear or follow anything you might happen to say. They may sneer, growl, glare, or furthermore, sigh deeply in exasperation at the sound of your voice or laughter. They are obnoxiously wrong in the way they treat us, and generally it is apparent to all. You almost want to ask, "What is wrong?" You cannot please this kind of person if you tried, as most have tried to please them without success. These guys are usually so embittered with their ex-wife that they have no respect for any woman, least of all, you.

This divorced man is a different case. The pastor himself needs to step into the place of protecting his wife. You do not need to have a confrontation with this kind of man. When my husband does that for me, I feel that I am highly valued in his eyes, and that keeps me from wanting to run, retreat, or fight back. It feels good when I do not have to defend myself to a man, but my husband does it for me.

The Lord has given us some trusted friends inside the church who know our hearts. From time to time, I have become a target, and when a man has tried to come against me, the board of elders will step in. They let him know that he is wrong, and they will not allow him to speak in that manner. The secret I have learned from King David is not to answer the accuser or fight for myself. We must allow God to do what He promises in His word. If we keep humble and keep our mouth shut, then the leaders can do their work. (Psalms 37 KJV)

I've Been There Before

There have been times when the old familiar contention concerning a woman preacher arises. Can she preach? Should she keep silent in the church? I am beyond that. After 31 years of preaching, it is enjoyable to share the pulpit with my husband on occasion and preach. I believe the key is to only preach when the Holy Spirit gives you a message for the body of believers that you pastor. Do not compete with your husband for the pulpit. My husband is the senior pastor, and I still listen very intently from the front row, my eyes on him, still receiving the word of God from him. Yes, I have heard most of his sermons before, but there is always a new anointing, a smile, a corny joke, and most of all, the love of God that permeates his messages. I am his greatest fan.

Women Preachers?

There have been men that have come up to me after I have given a message or exhortation, crying and saying, "I do not believe in women preachers, but what you just said had so much anointing and impact on my life, I cannot fight you or God."

I have personally struggled with this for years; I know I am called to be a minister of the Gospel of Jesus Christ. It burns deep in my soul. I try to do many things in the church to fulfill that Call. I will teach Wednesday night pre-teen class. I teach Women's Bible study on Thursday mornings. I have established my own ministry called "Hearts Afire" where periodically I preach to women. I have been the administrator/professor of our Bible College. I am the administrator for Restoring the Foundation Ministry. I am on the board of Manna for Life Outreach and occasionally work there.

I just listed for you all the major things I do, and I try my best to do them. But my Call is to preach the gospel of Jesus Christ and operate in the nine gifts of the Holy Spirit. This is one of the hardest things I have to accomplish to please God. The reason being is that I put my soul out there for others to either accept me or reject me. This is a hard position to be in when you just don't want to rock the boat because you never know how the people will respond. The people love it when you do all the things they do not want to do, but to speak into their lives, well, that's another matter.

Girls, I am not out to make a name for myself. I am out to be obedient to the call of God in my own life. Some of you came by this position because of your husband, but some of you came with the same fire of conviction being called to preach just like your husband. Never be ashamed of that Call. It is so precious. It will keep you going in the hard times of life when nothing seems to be working right.

Some of you are called to minister to your husband as he ministers to the church and that is fine, although the call can extend to you even though you do not feel it is yours. I know that a husband needs to know that his wife and family support the ministry. It is important that you do not talk down about his call by calling it, "his church, his work, his people." Statements like these can make a man feel alone in his call. I personally believe that when the man is called to pastor, that inside of this call, the woman has a responsibility to pick up her portion and be the helpmeet. I have never heard of God making a mistake in that area; when he calls the man, the woman should follow suit. Paul says to adapt yourself to your husband and walk into the call of pastoring together with God, because a three-braided cord is not easily broken. *"And if one prevail against him, two shall withstand him; and a threefold cord is not quickly broken."* (Eccl. 4: 12 KJV*) "In like manner you married women, be submissive to your own husbands – subordinate yourselves as being secondary to and dependent on them, and adapt yourselves to them. So that even if any do not obey the Word (of God), they may be won over not by discussion but by the (godly) lives of their wives."* (I Peter 3:1 Amp.)

Ladies, when you are having problems with a certain man inside the church, please let your husband know so that he can watch out for you. Let the husband notify the elders of your church to also be on the look out for anyone who would try to harm the pastor's wife. You will know when it is time to step back and let someone else minister to a divorced man or someone who is opposing you. Ladies, minister to the women and let the men pick up the slack. It is not your responsibility to correct a man that is contentious; you are to stay safe. Eventually, that person will either change or leave the church, and if he raises too many contentions, the elders are there to correct and see that he abides by the ordinances of the church.

I have had men come into the church that have been excited about the move of God in our church and really happy that God uses me from time to time. I have had a certain man come in and loudly proclaim in the foyer, "Pastor Sandy, I love you!" Then, after a little while, the newness wears off. I am still the same person I was when he darkened the doors and first came in, but now he is against me with fury. Oh, thank God for my elders and the young men in the church who treat me as a spiritual mother. They are not fooled by the opportunist and keep a watchful eye out for me. I am so proud of the men in our church; they are there for us. I do not have to be tough, because God has raised sons and daughters to come up along side of us to see that nothing happens to us. This is a very good feeling.

On the Flip Side

On the flip side of this (men who do not like women preachers, or ignore the pastor's wife for whatever ill feelings they may have against women), I also have experienced where several men were infatuated with me. I'll never forget the time that my husband did his normal, "Get out of your seat and greet your neighbor." That seemed innocent enough, and I was glad to visit with the others. However, this time a young man was seated in the back, and when I went to say hello, he took me in his arms and held me real tight. I was dumbfounded; my body was smacked up against his, and it was evident he was getting some kind of thrill in holding me in that position. I felt so shocked and then violated; he would not quit looking at me throughout the service. I told my husband when it happened, and he said he would look out for the young man. The next time we had church my husband again asked us to greet our neighbors. The young man was there and caught my eye. He was coming to give me another compromising hug. I shook my head "no." He shook his head, "yes." I again shook my head "no," but he kept coming. I turned and walked onto the platform, out the side door and went home. After church, he was corrected and never came close to me again. Times like that will put a chill in our veins, girls. No one wants to be in that position.

Pow! Right in the Kisser!

I remember the time a man wanted to kiss me, since the Bible instructs to greet each other with a kiss. (Romans 16:16 KJV) He would come to church, pucker up his lips and close his eyes right in front of my face. He would repeat the scripture and say, "Pastor Sandy, are you going to obey the Word of God?" I was quite disgusted with his behavior. It was neither genuine, nor called for. Finally, I became quite irritated and threatened him in front of his wife, who thought it was a joke. I told him, "If you do not quit harassing me, I will slug you right in the kisser!" Now, how lady-like or godly is that? I guess the tomboy in me got the best of me, although I did not hit him. I do not mind men kidding or joking with me, but they need to watch what they think they can say, or do to a pastor's wife. This particular man later repented for his rude behavior. Girls, we are not there to be the butt of their jokes or jesting. I live a holy life and expect people to treat me as such. I will not listen to any course joking or sexual innuendos because it is simply unacceptable. You set the boundaries, girls, and allow the pastor and elders to help enforce them. This will bring you peace.

I Was All Alone but Had a Phone!

I was in my office one Wednesday night. The service had already begun, when an angry man burst through the office door. My office was about six feet from the outside door, so he could actually come into my office without being noticed by the ushers. I happened to be seated when the man intruded upon my peace. He hit the door screaming at me, threatening my life and saying he was going to shut down the church. He said he was going to the police and have us arrested for being a cult. This man was serious. If Jesus would have been there and asked, "What is your name?" this man would have answered, "My name is murder, anger, and hatred!" The look in his eyes was unforgettable; I was looking into eyes of a demonic-oppressed man who was now looming over my desk (this is when I thank God I was raised by a tough drill sergeant!)

As he was spitting out the threats, I called his bluff and picked up the phone. I do not know how or why I knew the number of the police station, but I did. Without taking my eye off the man I dialed the number and spoke to a police officer. "There is a man here who is threatening my life and the safety of the church; he is coming over to make a formal complaint." The man was so surprised that I would do such a thing because he was used to manipulating people with his hatred and anger. I never saw him again.

I felt sorry for his wife. She lived with a man who continually used threats to control her. If I ever saw someone who was emotionally and verbally abused, it was her. At times she would sneak over to the church when we were having special meetings, but we were off limits to her if she wanted to be free from harassment.

I felt in control of the situation when it happened, but afterwards my heart was pounding and my body was shaking. I guess I realized that I was in danger, and there was nobody to defend me. It happened so quickly it was hard to explain. He would have been the type that would go to get a shotgun out of the trunk of his car and shoot up the church filled with the saints. That is a scary thought.

Girls, Please Pray With Me

Dear Lord, there are so many issues that I could bring up. There are those who have hurt me, lied about me, and showed me disrespect. I forgive them. I ask you to wash away all the hurt and disappointment in my life from those who deliberately tried to stop me, stifle me, and slander me. Please give me strength to not bow my knee to what they think of me. Give me a new look at myself in your eyes, Father. I have heard what man says about me, and now I need a fresh insight on how you see me. Help me to change the things that need to change and accept who I am in you, not in what the people say I am.

Renew my Call once again; give me the strength and ability to fulfill the Call you have placed on my life. I ask you to take away the fear of man, even his very look. Help me to seek and walk in your will for my life with all gentleness and submission to You and my husband. I want to be obedient to what you have placed in my life to do. I pray that you will give my husband wisdom to know and trust in my abilities as a trusted helpmeet. Let him be able to put the stamp of approval on what you have called me to do. I want your approval most of all Lord. I will not look or wait for man's approval. I will be obedient to your call, Lord. In Jesus' name, Amen.

Chapter 8

Hey Girls, Are the People Praying for You or Preying on You?

Smiles

We have had some wonderful people in our church over the years who have truly loved us. They have stood beside us through all types of successes and storms. They were always there with a smile, whether it was smile saying, "I understand and I am praying for you," or "I am proud of you and what God has done," or "Here comes Pastor Sandy, she's an easy target for teasing" (which I enjoy and can give back to those that often show affection by joking around.) There are smiles of those who truly respect us as their spiritual leaders and want to submit to pastoral guidance.

I love the little ones who were born since their parents started coming to church. They will run with open arms toward me, thinking I must be one of their grammas, since they see me at least two times per week. At any given time, there may be a child who runs to me and hugs my leg, waiting for me to hug them or smile at them. They do not understand that I am wearing my good Sunday clothes when they come rushing at me with chocolate donut hands. I love this great feeling and anyway, the clothes will wash. I love people of all ages and find satisfaction in engaging them in conversation. They all have so much to add to the church and to my life personally.

Let the Elders Pray

Girls, there are people in your church who genuinely pray for you, knowing the proper steps to pray for their pastors/leaders. We have an elder in our church who faithfully leads a prayer for us at Thursday morning prayer time. I can count on him to be wise and consider our lives and what we are going through at the moment; he prays effectively. When he prays for us and for our children, he does not use any judgmental prayers. He blesses us and asks God to uphold us, to give us health and to make our way prosperous. He asks the Lord to give us all wisdom to do His will, and he rebukes any unseen forces that would come at us to destroy or stop our ministry and relationship with God, our family and the people of our congregation. He prays for long life and for sickness and disease to remain at bay. When this elder prays, he is observing the times and seasons we, as leaders, our family, and the congregation are going through. He is a man of true integrity who knows how to pray the effectual fervent prayer of a righteous man. I know I am safe in those prayers of the elders. Thanks, Cletus.

When You Pray, Pray This

When you pray for your pastors, pray God's will according to what the Bible says about them. Pray the Scriptures according to New Testament standards. Paul wrote some wonderful, fulfilling prayers that you could insert the name of your pastors and family into it. This is a safe prayer. A wonderful book is *Praying God's Will for My Pastor* by Lee Roberts. When you pray for them, pray that Jesus would keep them well and blessed. Pray that God gives them wisdom and counsel.

Do not pray that they change their mind about something, especially if it concerns you and decisions they need to make. Do not pray your will upon them. Do not pray any prayer for them or their family which has words about cursing them and not letting them rest until they think it is the will of God. This is a curse. God will not fulfill these words, but the devil loves to help ignorant Christians praying things that are none of their concern. No one invited you into their life for you to curse them by the name of Jesus.

Pet Peeves

Can I share a pet peeve of mine? It is when people tell me they prayed my son or daughter would not succeed in a secular career, but rather to fail at everything until they take up the call that is on their parent's life. Leave this to God. Do not interfere with the plans and purpose of God. Girls, be certain not to let people get away with these types of prayers.

This leads me to the other side of the people praying for their pastors/pastors' wives. Let me ask you a few questions:

- Girls, have you ever felt like something was wrong, but you could not put your finger on it?
- Have you ever felt like you were in a battle, but did not know the source?
- Have you ever felt or sensed that you had a big decision to make, but felt confusion and frustration?
- Have you ever felt or experienced "outside" pressure, but you did not know where it came from?
- Have you ever felt or knew that people were praying their will upon you?

Many pastors' wives fall prey to other people's prayers. Sometimes, instead of the people having the ability to pray God's wisdom and understanding for you, they will begin a "campaign" of praying what they want you to do or change. This is not a fun place to be in. Yes, we can always have room for improvement. However, it is insulting to us, especially when we are doing our best to stay within the guidelines of what we believe is the "plan of God."

I can tell you that some people will "prey/pray" to knock you out of your leadership role, so they can conveniently take over your position. I know this sounds paranoid, but anytime a hierarchy of power of any kind exists, somebody will want your position, particularly so if you are a woman in ministry with authority. This happens in the world system all the time! I believe it is called a "take over."

Some people may not care if your husband carries the authority, but they will want to keep that authority out of your hands! It is amazing how this abuse may operate in the church. Some are "undercurrents." They really don't say much to you, but you can "feel it" in their presence. At times, you would think there is a horde of pirates on the loose, ready to commandeer your church. (Hebrews 12:15 KJV)

Sometimes when you feel so pressured, you may become despondent and wonder if it is worth it. Women of God, if God truly placed you in authority along with your husband, I promise you it is worth it. Do not pull back. Do not give in to the pressures of false prayers. I know there are times in our lives when we gladly relinquish our responsibilities. I rejoice at those opportunities more than ever if I know someone will do a good job and that they are already trustworthy and loyal. It makes a big difference when the Holy Spirit and the Word of God frowns upon someone trying to push you out of position for his or her own selfish gain. For the sake of the rest of the believers, it is our duty to identify it and put a stop to it.

I am not astonished at how some would like to have a position of authority that they can neither handle, nor will the people follow. It is like playing with fire: it burns and it scars. Nothing is worse than a church hurt. The ministry is nothing to take lightly, yet some think they can do it better than you can. Perhaps they can, but it is not theirs to do or to have. Ladies, this is our position, our field to glean, our ministry, our mandate, our calling and our job description. The Holy Spirit assigned us to the task and it is our five talents the master gave us to multiply. (Matthew 25:14-30 KJV)

Who Bullied You Out of Your Position?

Girls, have you ever felt like you do not "fit?" Who is praying for you? How are they praying? What has been taken out of your hands? Was your assignment over? Was it timing or did someone, somehow usurp your authority by using the words, "God said"? Did they do you a "favor," or did God say, or was it the power of suggestion? Did they bully you out of your position? Whether it's "prey-ors" or prayers, it is not the people's place to tell you what God says. Only your husband and you must know the plan of God for you.

It is such a blessing when the husband/pastor blesses his wife and releases her into ministry or into a career, or when he releases her to be the domestic engineer of the home to care for him and the family.

There have been major times when Dennis has confirmed and reaffirmed the call of God on my life. I have been on the mountaintop, and I have been in the valley low. I have been in an uneventful place where life is mediocre and mundane. It is a priceless blessing when your husband can come up alongside you and give words of encouragement. What a difference that makes since he is the spiritual head over you and over the church.

Let Your Husband Pray a Blessing Over You

When your husband believes in you and the call of God on your life, it makes all the difference. I treasure the letters Dennis has written to me over the years, and the times he has taken me in his arms to bless me before I preach. He is proud of me, and when he introduces me to the congregation, I am either going to become teary eyed or totally embarrassed by his grand introduction of his wife. He truly honors and respects my place in ministry. He trusts me and relies on me to "hear from the Holy Spirit." We make a great team.

I am not in competition with my husband's role as the senior pastor. I want to complement and be his helpmeet. I do not act as one who has to know every move the man makes. I do not have to preach two to three times per month so that I have equal time. I do not need that, nor does the church (a little of me goes a long way). My husband is a quiet, gentle man, filled with wisdom and ability. I know I am a strong force. A long time ago, we realized that he needed to increase his authority, and I needed to decrease mine. At the beginning of our pastoral ministry, we agreed that I would work at a secular job, and he would be at the church office to do the work of the ministry.

It has worked well for us. I did not lose out in anointing by doing this; I did not lose my ability to preach. Instead, I went into another dimension of the anointing. That is, Dennis took the full lead, and I follow (as much as I am able to.) This has freed us to do what the Lord has called both of us to do. For years now, we have worked at the church together. I do the work he cannot and will not do, which is extended counseling and minor decision-making in the everyday operation of the church.

The Bible says pastors are to be devoted to prayer and the Word. Dennis loves both. There is not a day that I do not see his nose in the Bible or hear him praying. He loves to worship the Lord in songs, singing and making melody in his heart to the Lord. When I feel my time may be up in extended counseling, he urges me to continue with the words, "The people need you and your team; I see great growth and strength in the ones you have ministered to in counseling." My husband/pastor sets the pace, and I try to willingly follow.

There are times I need more convincing, so I take it to prayer and to Him directly. I do not want to just do good things for the kingdom, but I want to be productive for the kingdom of God. When you submit yourself to God and to your husband, you will be right where God wants you and there will be peace. I know that sometimes God has turned the corner and your husband kept going on the same path that he has been on for awhile. There is such a safety in the same routine, but in those times we need to have the ability to speak to our husbands and question them concerning what they think God is doing. It is time to review the vision, goals, and dreams.

I wish I could say that husbands know everything, and that they are always right when leading the wife, the family and the church. It is untrue that they must have that heavy burden put solely on them. That is why God gave him a helpmeet: his wife knows him better than anyone else. When you leave it all for him to face, it can be a very lonely place. He has to be able to vent or express what he is going through. Your husband needs to be heard not just as the man of God with the message of the hour. We need to take a genuine interest in what he is doing and planning. The call of God first came to the husband and wife team and that is where the main stream flows out to the elders and advisory board.

Go to Your Closet!

When writing of prayer, I would be remiss if I did not mention that you as a pastor's wife (in whatever capacity you carry with your husband, whatever agreements you have worked out between the two of you, in the ministry, secular career, or caring for the home) must be praying. Be a person of prayer and let others in the church know that you believe in and like to, pray and practice prayer.

When a husband and wife are going through a battle, it is good to know how to pray. What we want from the congregation should be for us as well. They do not hold a market on praying ineffectively; we need to learn to give enough respect that we teach them. I know pastors' prayers are different and many times, I cannot share my heart with the people. I may know more than they do concerning a situation, and I need my privacy to pray.

I will go to the intercessory prayer group, but I know better than to give secrets away through open prayer. This can be devastating to a person in the congregation if we have revealed what they are going through without permission. You want to talk to God about a need in a person's life, but when it becomes a form a gossip and hearsay, dear pastor's wife, find a new way of praying.

Go to your secret closet and pray, revealing nothing to others. Do not twist it about so that this becomes your opinion of that person. Say the prayer request and pray the prayer. Do not be prejudiced, and do not give away information that was only meant for you. You will find yourself being accused of not being able to keep a confidence.

Another thing I do is I never talk to the person I am counseling with through prayer and teaching the Word, in the hallway, foyer, bathroom, sanctuary, etc. I let them know that what I minister is for the prayer ministry room, not for other people to hear as they were walking by. This is inappropriate and can cause embarrassment and hurt feelings.

When you have taken on the pastoral role along with your husband, the burden of knowing much information is necessary. One reason is to pray and to plan what to do with the people who are struggling with life and sin. It is our duty to be watchmen on the wall and pray for their best interest. We must know how to pray warfare prayers and stand in the gap for that dear one going through a trial. These are an ongoing responsibilities, and I thank God for the elders who are set in place and take that burden along with us. We are mighty in pulling down of strongholds when we pray for some individuals. (II Corinthians 10:1-8 KJV) Sometimes it does not seem things are changing from our viewpoint, but that is God's business to deal with them. At times, it becomes ours, since we are the ones that have to discipline and bring them back into alignment with the Word of God and the plan of God for the church and their life.

If you have an inner circle of trusted elders who need to know what is happening so they can also pray, be sure to set the example and establish the prerequisite that this is not to be talked about nor hinted at among other people. There should be no rolling of the eyes with disgust or an "issue" taken care of (discipline) immediately, when prayer had not taken place first. If we had jumped the gun, we would have eventually lost a good member of the church by reason of prejudging and not praying. Be very selective of whom you bring into the inner circle of prayer and the information you give them.

Pastors' wives, it is easy to fall into this trap of knowing too much and having to let another know personal information in the disguise of a prayer request. Many times, this will backfire on you. Know who labors among you and whom you can trust. Do not let it be a priority with you to have to give the latest information out to a few close friends about something going on in the church. You can create a faction. Never let it be said that the pastor's wife is the culprit who creates division and distrust in the church. Go to the closet!

I know we may become very burdened with some of the stress in the ministry. It is not good to confide in the church members for this. I remember the scripture about how men were coming against David. His instructions were not to defend himself, but to keep his mouth shut. I have been caught with my mouth open, maybe not to the people, but to God. The Holy Ghost has a way of letting you know that you have sinned! It is time to repent when this happens; it will not do you any good to try to justify your actions or your words. You might as well cry for mercy because you are guilty according to the Word of God. Oh, this is not a pleasant subject, but it happens to all people that the Holy Ghost caught up to before they made a disaster out of things inside the church. Thank God for those who are around you, for those who have grace and mercy on you and will pray for you to handle this correctly.

If you cannot take care of this matter in prayer and confrontation alone, please find yourself a Spirit-filled pastoral couple that is seasoned in the ministry. I find great joy to go to another pastoral couple who has been around for some time. They may have a few battle scars, but they have a sweet spirit and can listen, advise, pray, and speak into your life to correct the matters that need to be corrected. Can you do that, or do you think because you are the pastor there is no room to correct the man and woman of God? Please realize that we all need to be accountable to others of like precious faith. I do not necessarily need someone to agree with me; I need a solution.

Just as we teach the people to humble themselves, we must be the first to do so and seek help. Frustration may build when the preacher you poured your heart out to does not agree with you, but sees both sides and lets you know that you could be to blame. Some preachers think they are untouchable when it comes to charges laid at their feet, or they feel they are above correction. What do we do with the Scripture that says if we are not chastened, then we cannot be His sons, but a bastard? (Hebrews 12:8 KJV) I know these are strong words, but sometimes we need someone to speak a strong word into our lives so that we know we are not exempt from doing wrong. Being wrong and therefore needing to humble ourselves before God first, then the man or woman of God you entrusted with this information, knowing that they would give you a fair evaluation of the problem. It is good if it never gets this far, but if it does, we should be able to take it, since we have given this advice many times to those we shepherd. They do not like it either, but I pray that they will take it in the love it was intended to shepherd them and lead them into paths of repentance.

Girls, we know the proper way of correcting a problem. We are to leave our gift at the altar and go to that person. If you need to forgive them, do so; if you can just take care of it without involving anyone else you have an excellent spirit. Ladies, just because you are having a problem with a person does not mean your friends have to know about it. Take it to the Lord first, and if you can take care of it by forgiving, then great.

Conversely, many times people do not even realize that they have hurt us, so therefore, why involve them at all? Have grace enough to let it go and move on; there does not have to be a discussion. However, if they have offended you, then go to them quickly. Do not brood over it; "go quickly" is what the Word says. I believe most arguments in the church could be avoided if we follow the Biblical guidelines and not share a prayer, which is really letting your girlfriends know that someone in the church crossed over the invisible line and offended you. We should realize that we ought to save it for the big battle the enemy of our soul has planned for us, instead of being entangled with these little skirmishes that do not matter.

The word is restoration. We need to be ministers of restoration, giving the people the opportunity to learn forgiveness. We do not have to be right all the time, nor will we have the correct answer for them all the time. They know we are human and need to see and hear that we are not their gods, but that we do make mistakes and ask them to forgive us. I think the key is not taking the one incident and letting it build up to the place that, when you finally get the courage or become angry enough, you go to the person with a whole laundry list of complaints. No one likes or can accept this type of treatment.

Dessert, Anyone?

I remember the time some people came to me with "their list." Wow, talk about a laundry list! I had no idea about half the stuff they were complaining about, and I certainly did not know I had offended anyone. To this day, I can remember when I went to a nice board member's house for dessert, where they descended upon me like vultures. Unbeknownst to me, this person invited a few people who had "problems" with me. She failed to understand that one of the people against me just happened to be an undiagnosed victim of the bipolar mental disorder, and the other was a Jezebel. (Ps. 41: 9 KJV)

I was so hurt and caught off guard. I remember just running into my husband's arms and crying so hard. We were both dumbfounded; because we thought we were in a safe place. It is amazing how certain types of people are literally out to get you and can take anything as innocent as a meeting with the pastors to talk and turn it into an ambush.

It took a long time before I was ever able to go to a house meeting for dessert. I now have very gracious friends who know some of our story, and they would not put us through a terrible ordeal like that again. God has given us some wonderful people with whom we can be transparent. It is good when your people are mature and can come to you one on one before trouble starts brooding.

I often wondered what could have been different. We were so young, and at that time did not know the heart of some people until they bit us. For many years afterwards, I would ask when invited to someone's home, "What is the meeting about, why do you want us there, and who else will be present?"

I now believe if you have anything to say to the pastors of such an explosive nature, you must meet the pastors and some elders at the office. Before anything is discussed, we will have an hour prayer meeting, praying in the Spirit and confessing our sins to God first. After prayer and personal and corporate confession, you can let me know what is wrong.

I do not believe there is enough prayer covering for such matters. There is too much talk and accusing. Let's confess our sins before God and forgive each other instead. Much of what is brought before the pastors will not mean anything once the dust is settled and they are searching for a new pastor.

Is it worth it to disrupt others in the congregation with the dissension that occurred because you did not like something? Such foolishness we have fallen into; the devil laid a trap into which we have fallen. How could we, as pastors' wives, have prevented this? Did we have something in our power to stop the dissension? Could we have overlooked "Sister So-and-So" and not have taken it to heart? Could we have forgiven her right away instead of forming a posse to make her life miserable? Did the clique you formed backfire on the pastor's wife? How do we get back on track?

By now, you are either mad at me or you are thinking that I am really hard on you. I have been in the ministry over 31 years, and I have heard many stories and made my own mistakes. I'm quite sure I will make more. We have the tools to fix it: the Word of God, the Holy Spirit, prayer, love, forgiveness, and humbling ourselves. I think sometimes we think it is us against the congregation. Yes, it seems that way at times, but that is just the ploy of the devil to get you to think it is hopeless. If we can remember that it is not about us, but about the church and that Christ died for us. The enemy wants us to get off track so that the whole church, not just the pastors, end up being the laughing stock of the world. Let me remind you that when Moses was on the assignment of bringing the Children of Israel out of Egypt, the people (his church) started murmuring and talking against God and the leadership. God told Moses, "Just get out of the way, I am going to destroy this bunch of ungrateful people, and I will start over with you." Moses stood in the gap and said, "Oh, do not let the devil laugh at us to think that you would go to such means to get them out of Egypt, only to destroy them out in the wilderness!"

Moses had a love for the people even though at times, he was so irate with them. That is how we are at times. We love them, but then become annoyed with them too. We feel they should have known better. In the times that we reveal ourselves to the people, it is nice when they can overlook our faults and pray for us. There are times we will have to go back and humble ourselves and ask them to forgive us. I did not read where Moses did this, but we must be good stewards of the full gospel. This makes us real when they see that we can get mad, but that we can repent if need be. We can be angry and sin not according to the Word, but I do not believe that we should make a habit of it. It is not becoming of a leader of God's people.

Can You Pray This Prayer With Me?

Dear God,

I confess that I have been so angry with the people. I have heard the prayers which they have ignorantly prayed over my family and me. They have said things that have hurt and offended me. It embarrasses me that they thought they could say harsh and critical words against my family and me in my presence and think it was acceptable. I forgive them for praying their will upon me. I forgive them for not considering my feelings. I forgive them for praying curses upon my family and me.

Father, I ask you to give us wisdom to teach the people how to pray properly and lovingly for their pastors. Please forgive me for my response to these people, for the times I have been mad and hurt and would not talk to them. Please forgive me for the times I would isolate myself and would not join them in corporate prayer. Please forgive me for carrying these hurts and wounds, not allowing you to heal me, but harboring resentments instead. Please forgive me for moving away from your people and from prayer. Renew my relationship with the people. I want to pray again without wrath or doubting. Lord, I ask you to put well-qualified pastors in my life that I can trust to speak truth to me and who will help me heal. Help me know when I need to forgive on my own or when I need to go to the person alone to take care of the matter. Give me the discretion to be a godly pastor's wife who knows how to pray and forgive without involving others. Let the Spirit of peace and godly contentment rest on me now, in Jesus' name. Amen.

Chapter 9

How Do You Protect Your Church?

I Didn't See It Coming!

We often feel clueless when we have been caught off guard with a major incident in the church. You feel as if you have lost the grip on your church. Jesus knew in advance this would happen. He gave more than enough instruction on how to deal with crisis in the church. Leaning upon the instructions Jesus gave us as a safe guard is essential.

It Makes You Want to Hang Your Head in Shame

Some of the stories I have heard about over the years can terrify the even strongest pastoral unit of the husband and wife team. The elder who would not renounce his hidden connections with the occult, he had to go. The music leader who is disqualified because of their porno addiction refused to seek help, dismissed. The youth pastor who was caught naked on the platform, in the middle of the day! The elder convicted of child abuse. The Church Treasurer who lost the church money gambling or other ways of mishandled church money, fired. The board of elders who conspired to destroy the pastor's life with accusation and slander, the family had to leave the church. Leaders caught in adultery. The pastor who ran away with the secretary and the money! The unforgiving spirit, misconduct and bad attitudes of the church leaders will destroy any chance of a Pastor bringing reconciliation to the church body. The examples are endless, and they are petrifying.

When Dennis and I have had trouble in our church, we tried to preface the problem with, 'this is not an everyday occurrence in our church. We have not been here before and so we ask for your patience.' Often years may go by before we have an "incident" where this type of discipline is exercised. We take our time to review each case and prayerfully search the Holy Scripture for what is correct in each case. We want to do what is right according to the Word of God, and not according to the "world system." I do not think the church (congregation) needs to know every gory detail.

We are to protect the babes in Christ, the family members of the person who sinned, and basically, the church. The gossip that can come from this type of discipline can be devastating and a disgrace to the body of Christ if it is allowed to be blown out of proportion.

Don't Be Afraid to Address the Issues

Girls, we as co-leaders need to know how to address these issues and see to it that discipline follows the incident. I do not want to be the ministry which sweeps the junk under the carpet and sends the offender to another area of the country so that they do not have to put up with the scandal. This does not help the person who has sinned. There must be confession and repentance of the sin. The offender must be willing to seek professional godly counsel and accept accountability. How can anyone be restored if we hide the sin? Without restoration, this sin will follow the man or woman. Do not set them up in another pastorate where they can practice the same sin again, especially if it is a sexual sin. Others being unaware of the sin will suffer, and you will be held accountable for the ensuing devastation.

Jesus and the apostles gave us some excellent instructions on how to address these issues inside the church. In Matthew 18, he addresses how to have healthy relationships. The church that Jesus refers to in Matthew 18 is depicted as a flock of one hundred sheep. The spiritual leaders, the under shepherd, (pastors) elders, and overseers are there to teach, watch, admonish, rebuke, reprove, correct, much like responsible parents. (Eph. 4:11-12; Titus 1:5 KJV)

Do Not Harm the Babies!

In Matthew 18:10, the Lord said to take heed, pay attention, and be aware that you do not harm the little ones, who are the lambs or babes in Christ. He is concerned for the safety and well-being of the little ones, as we also should be. We automatically take a baby in our arms and love on them. They offer us nothing but trust and want to hear us speak good and loving words to them. Likewise, with a babe in Christ, we should be excited that they are learning how to talk, walk, and take care of some of their own needs.

Jesus loved the sheep no matter their age. When one of the sheep left, Jesus, the Shepherd of our soul, willingly left the ninety-nine, to find the one. Jesus made it very clear how important it is to love and not take your anger out on the little ones. Picture a lamb (babe in Christ) who is scolded or condemned by a supposedly mature Christian. This lamb received a tongue lashing which stung so badly that either they left the church entirely or would not enter a certain area of ministry, all because of the well-meaning saint who showed no patience or understanding. The saint forgot where they came from and how long it took them to mature. The "mature ones" have gotten it in their head that they are the policeman, the regulator and the law keeper. They usually operate without mercy. They speak much "Christian-ease" and totally confuse and intimidate the babe in Christ. When this happens, they need to have a new dip of the Holy Ghost in their life, so that they can become sweet again.

Girls, have you ever seen a toddler try to wear his daddy's shoes? He carefully inches his way around the room and eventually falls. The shoes are too big, and the little guy cannot fit into them nor keep his balance. That's what raising babies is all about, BALANCE. They need routine, small meals of nutritious foods and regular changing so that they are not infected with sickness and disease. They need lots of love and a tender voice, along with soft eyes to look back at them.

They do not need to see a pair of disapproving eyes on them when they enter the area where the "watchdog" of the church resides. Give the little ones a break so they can grow without fear and condemnation. You cannot expect them to grow overnight. We are not to shove food down their throat, but instead we must give them the milk of the Word. I've seen the babe in Christ that the older ones got hold of to "enlighten." No, they are not ready for that stuff. If you feed them all the 'hype,' and there are many 'hypes' in churches, it is like giving them candy three times per day as their meal. It's evident when you find a child living on sweets. They are hyper, they cannot settle down, and it is hard for them to hear or pay attention. Now think about a newborn believer who has gotten off to a bad start by hanging around those who wanted to show him a good time by taking him to church services that are so fanatical that all he learns is to be fanatical. Once they get a taste of the 'hype,' it is as if they are ruined for any normal kind of Christian life, which enjoys the simple meat and potatoes of the Word of God. They keep moving from church to church and never settle down. Paul said to Timothy, a young pastor *preach sound doctrine*. Yes there will always be the 'hype', but we learn by hearing sound doctrine and following the practices of it. *"As newborn babes, desire the sincere milk of the word that ye may grow thereby."* (1 Peter 2:2 KJV)

If we could see past the size and age of the person without patronizing them and consider them as babies or toddlers, we would see their need of being nurtured and guided to maturity. In the church it is not good to allow children (new converts) to grow without supervision, but we are excited for the 'new life' that is birthed through salvation. We celebrate as the angels do in heaven when someone is born again, understanding that they have asked forgiveness of their sins. Now the sin needs to get out of their life! (Luke 15:10 KJV)

How to Care For a Baby Christian

Every baby Christian needs to receive a good, solid teaching of the Bible. They realize that they have received a new identity unlike their former way of living. It takes time for them to form new beliefs and put off the old ungodly beliefs and nature. (Rom. 12:2; Eph. 4:22-23; Col. 3:9-10 KJV). Along with being under good Bible-based teaching, the baby Christian needs to be able to read and understand the Bible for himself. It is good to have a plan for the person to read through the New Testament. *Thy word have I hid in mine heart, that I might not sin against thee."* (Ps 119:11 KJV) Learn to pray with all types of prayers. When he learns that he can have a personal relationship with his Lord and Father God through the Holy Spirit, it can change him forever. Teach and encourage them to pray daily. If you teach them to start and end the day in prayer, this will help them tremendously to know that the Lord delights in hearing them pray and that the answers are on the way. (Eph. 6: 18 KJV)

Take time to connect a baby Christian with an elder who is apt to teach as a gentle and patient parent. When you connect them with those who can influence them and help them grow, a friendship will develop. As they become friends, it will be hard for them to slip through the revolving doors of the church.

Sheep Bites

After Jesus warns the disciples concerning the "little ones.' He begins the second part of his teaching concerning relationships of believers. Matthew 18: 15 *Moreover if thy brother shall trespass against thee*. "Trespass" is a very strong word. It actually means to miss the mark, to sin against someone, to offend morally, to make a moral failure concerning someone else.

Girls, this is not about petty and immature complaints concerning others or things such as we did not shake the hand of sister so-and-so in church. As pastors' wives, it is amazing how many times people become offended at us rather than at the pastor. They rationalize that the pastor is the man of God and very busy preparing for the sermon. We, on the other hand, are sitting ducks. The pastor's wife is often seen as the offending party, which leaves us in a place where we are vulnerable to the attacks of the sheep.

We attended a special church service where the preacher prayed for the pastors' wives who had suffered "sheep bites." At first, I was caught off guard by the wording, but then realized that this happens far too often. I do not know how many times I have been told I offended someone. They felt that I had intentionally slighted them or made a decision that they did not care for. Instead of them coming to talk to me about it, they bit me in the back!

Now some may say, "Well Pastor Sandy, if you would just do such and such, this would not happen." And for all you girls who are so very careful to never offend a sheep, it still happens. You cannot be held accountable for other people's actions towards you. We go into a performance mode all too often. We are not being ourselves. We take on the fear of man, and we suddenly find that we cannot relax because we have become fearful of the sheep. Perhaps we did not shake one of their hands, pat their baby, or ask about a sick loved one. This can be a real pressure on us, and we may go home wondering if we failed to give all we needed to give to the people.

The devil loves to wreak havoc on us, particularly in our emotions. Especially if the people were here one Sunday and then absent the next two Sundays, we cannot help but wonder what we could have said or not said that would bring them back and keep them faithful to the house of God.

At this point, I would just like to burst out in song, "I gotta be me!" I love people and want them to know it. I do have a genuine interest in the people. That is me! I love that about me, and I do not want to manufacture something out of an obligation to "meet the need and keep the sheep." I know some of you suffer with the very thought that you have to be in the public eye and try to visit with many of the people in the church. . Or perhaps you have recently been sheep bit and are trying to recover from the last episode. This can be distressing for you especially if you feel that you are failing in this area.

Take a deep breath, girls. We will *never* meet all the needs of the sheep. After all, it is not our responsibility. The Lord is depending upon their faithfulness to the house of God. We are blessed if we see them at the most two times per week. I cannot count the times I said out loud to my husband and the Lord, "If the Lord does not build the house, our labor is in vain." This releases me from any false expectations I, my husband or anyone else tries to put on me.

I Would Be a Millionaire if . . .

I would actually be a millionaire, not to mention excessively bitter, if I had a dollar for every time someone looked at me crossed-eyed or spoke my name in a derogatory manner. This could be my retirement plan. Too bad I did not think of this at the very beginning. The key would be that you would pay yourself a dollar each time a trivial offense took place. Then as you forgive and release the person from any type of retribution, you get to keep the dollar.

We are experienced with the look, the snubbing, the skirting around, the ignoring, or the telling of close friends so that they join in their crusade to punish the offender. Do yourself a favor, find a very pretty box. Keep it where you can see it daily and when you make the decision to forgive and forget throw a dollar in the box. Pay yourself dividends which only God can bless. Remember, do not give yourself a dollar for every hurt, but for every time you forgive and see that it is resolved. Take your husband on a date night or save that cash for a get away.

If Offended with Someone who Sinned Against You

Let us not use this out of the context of church discipline. Instead of telling the other person their fault, first see if you can solve it without their knowledge.

- John 15:12, we are instructed to **love.**
- Matt. 7:1-2, we are instructed **not to judge** and we are forewarned of consequences.
- Heb. 12:15, we are warned of the root of bitterness that can spring up within us. We need to **walk in grace.**
- Col. 3:12,13, we need to **clothe ourselves** with compassion, kindness, humility, meekness, longsuffering, forbearance and forgiveness.
- Phil. 2:3-4, we must not do things for vain glory but because of love **prefer others.**

Realize that there is an extensive list of many important scriptures on Christian conduct. Our responsibility is to instruct the sheep/people, so that they can understand what to do and how to respond in different circumstances. Test the heart first and try to come to some sort of settlement on your own, before you take steps which include others. "Search me, O God, and know my heart: try me, and know my thoughts." (Ps. 139: 23 KJV)

If My Brother Trespasses Against Me

> *Moreover if thy brother shall trespass against thee, go and tell him his fault between thee and him alone: if he shall hear thee, thou hast gained thy brother.* (Matthew 18:15 KJV)

Girls, when you find yourselves 'trespassed against,' go to that person and clear up the matter. Then you win your brother back. Realize that this is not a one-way street. When you tell them their fault, do not neglect to ask them for forgiveness for how you responded. Too many people are hurt in this process because of our response. They may feel the need to defend themselves or even deny the problem completely. We all perceive things differently, and we must yield if we can. Thayer's Greek-English Lexicon of the New Testament says it this way, "go and tell him his fault between thee and him alone: To call into account, show one his fault, demand an explanation from someone."

In Matthew 5: 23-24, we realize that the Lord speaks to us through the Word of God we have in our hearts. The Holy Spirit then impresses us not to offer the gift until we have made it right with the offended brother. *"And Samuel said, Hath the Lord as great delight in burnt offerings and sacrifices, as in obeying the voice of the Lord? Behold, to obey is better than sacrifice, and to hearken than the fat of rams."* (I Samuel 15: 22 KJV)

This truth that God loves obedience more than sacrifice causes us to take a good look at our conduct as we go to the one who has offended us. Stay meek when bringing the offense to the other person. This attitude carries great weight and may convey your sincerity. Your tone of voice, the expression of the face, and the body language can set the mood for the whole session. It is hard to relax once you have taken the stance that you are going to clear this matter up. Gestures such as your hand on your hip, your crossed arms, the scowl on your face, are threatening gestures sure to intimidate the other person. Any attempt to "straighten out" your brother should not be considered until you have prayed about this and have removed the beam from your own eye. I know all you really want to do is tell him off for how badly he hurt you. But please, you must be a peacemaker and not alienate your brother.

Choose Your Battles Wisely

Be wary that this kind of confrontation may backfire. What you thought would be one-sided may have a double-edged sword effect. Once they have heard you and your complaint of them, consequently it is their turn to express how they feel. I am always amazed by how much is stored up inside of a person against others. Many have never released any of the misdemeanors but have "collected evidence" along the way. Their hearts are storage tank for hazardous waste. Now suddenly you may find the subject blown out of proportion with disastrous results. Remember this is why Jesus instructs us to get it done now, not later, so that people do not brood over the offense.

Now that the tables are turned on you, you can redeem this time by not taking offense yourself. Just as some do not know that they have offended you, it can be just as true for you to not understand that you have hurt or offended the other. When this happens, humbly listen to the complaints, being careful not to interrupt with self-defenses. With a meek and quiet spirit, apologize for your actions. Let them know you never meant to hurt them, and then ask them for forgiveness. Wait for them to respond with "I forgive you."

Girls, remember that it is hard to go back to the same quality relationship you enjoyed prior to the hurt and confrontation. The wounds of a friend are precious, but it does indeed still hurt. (Pro. 27:6 KJV) Time is a necessity to heal these wounds. The time depends upon personality and how well people recover from any type of confrontation. Keep in mind that this is when the devil slips in with rejection, fear and anger. The hurt person may rehearse the whole incident over in their mind. Suddenly they may feel as if the church has spiritually abused them. Some may feel like the pastor/ shepherd did not protect them. Some may feel unwanted. They seem to drift away from the church, since they cannot forget the pain of the wound, no matter if it was resolved. Healing of the wounded heart is a must. As Jesus explained in Luke 4: 18: "The Spirit of the Lord is upon me, because he hath anointed me to preach the gospel to the poor; he hath sent me to heal the brokenhearted, to preach deliverance to the captives, and recovering of sight to the blind, to set at liberty them that are bruised, 19; To preach the acceptable year of the Lord." (KJV)

It's imperative that we know that He came to bind up our wounds as well. Sometimes we are so busy saving the sheep that we forget to look at the wounds oozing from our wounded heart. At times we do not even know about it until we are in crisis state. We are infected with bitterness, stress, and weariness.

Please Know My Heart

The main objective of discipline is for the person to "hear you and to understand the complaint." If our efforts to repair the offense are futile, it is our responsibility to take up the matter scripturally. If we find the person will not listen or hear us, the word actually means "to understand the complaint." This may take some doing, but if any person gets angry and nothing is resolved, it then should go before two or three witnesses. (Deuteronomy 19:15; II Cor. 13:1 KJV)

These witnesses are not there to take sides. Their duty is to spiritually discern what each party is trying to convey and bring peace to the situation. In this way, it is not your word against someone else. "He that answereth a matter before he heareth it, it is folly and shame unto him." (Prov 18:3 KJV) The Word instructs us not to agree with one person until we have heard both sides of the story. What someone calls sin or transgression could be a mere matter of opinion. The witnesses should be people of integrity, wisdom, and maturity that both people trust, knowing that their rights and feeling will be protected as much as possible. These witnesses can monitor the actions and words of both parties and regulate the tone of voice, keeping the meeting quiet and private. If we can manage this, we can save a brother from a tremendous fall by treating him with fairness, love and honor.

Too many times, these scenarios turn into witch-hunts or lynch mobs. This kind of treatment is a disgrace to the church and should never happen. To our shame, this has happened in the church. People have been "ambushed" in the pastor's office, and now if you ask them to come into the office for a private visit, they immediately start to tremble inside or take on the offensive in order to protect themselves from a potential attack. Let us remember that sheep may have been beaten by pastors in the past.

Every Sin has a Consequence

Sometimes, a person may choose not to listen to the witnesses and resolve the situation based on their recommendations. What then? Then issue is taken before the church. When bringing someone before the church, you better know what the Bible teaches. It is wise to have your church by-laws state that you correct and discipline according to the Word of God. It is imperative that we clarify and understand the offense and know what the Bible says about it. Of course, we have to check our heart's attitude and the Word of God for direction when an individual comes to this place in their life. Some of the problems that would lead to this type of discipline would be:

- A trespass (Greek: sin, note, Jn. 1:29) plus an unforgiving spirit (Mt. 18:15-17)
- False doctrines and offenses contrary to Scripture (Rom. 16:17)
- Hating Christ (I Cor. 16:22)
- Disorderly conduct and disobedience (II Th. 3:6,14-15)
- Apostasy (I Tim. 1:19-20; 4:1-8; II Tim. 3:5; 4:1-4)
- Heresy (Tit. 3:10; I Tim. 6:3-5)
- Fornication and other gross sins that damn the soul (I Cor.; 6:9-11; Gal. 5:19-21; Mk. 7:21-23; Rom. 1:18-32; Col. 5:5-10; I Tim. 6:3-5) [28]

This process is demonstrated when the Jerusalem church heard rumors of what Paul and his companions were practicing by allowing the Gentiles to come to Christ without circumcision and by allowing the eating of meat that may have been offered to idols. Instead of allowing the leaders to wonder about this, Paul went to Jerusalem and gave a report of the ministry. Remember, Paul was new on the block and under scrutiny by Judaizers. The reports came back when they visited with the council there, and they found that all the accusations were false. The council asked them to obey certain guidelines, and Paul and his men said they already practiced it and would submit to them. Who could ask for anything more? They continued to work for the Lord in peace with their spiritual leaders:

> *Verily I say unto you, whatsoever ye shall bind on earth shall be bound in heaven: and whatsoever ye shall loose on earth shall be loosed in heaven. 19. Again I say unto you, That if two of you shall agree on earth as touching any thing that they shall ask, it shall be done for them of my Father which is in heaven. 20 for where two or three are gathered together in my name, there am I in the midst of them* (Matt. 18: 18-20 KJV)

Sometimes I wonder if we have taken this out of context to prove our authority to pray and agree. On the other hand, is this actually continuing with the same subject, which is discipline? Is this our legal right as church government to follow this set of Scriptures, which we deem holy and God breathed? He gives us authority to examine Scripture and to make judgments of what we will allow in the church according to His Word, but not according to that of which we approve. It is a safe guard from the world's system which thinks what we believe as a church is archaic and obsolete.

Since we became senior pastors, I can count on one hand how many times church discipline was successfully accomplished and the person actually accepted the decision of the church. Too many people leave the church. They rebel and let the church know that there are other pastures with grass that is much more inviting at this time. Oh, that has been a tremendous loss to the church when people will not allow correction, so that they may learn and be able to be restored.

He was Caught!

Just the other day, a person was caught in the illicit habit of pornography and cross dressing. The first time he was confronted, he confessed, repented, and tried to reform. The pastors watched him closely and put him on probation. However, the ugly sinning perpetuated. The man was immediately removed from the music team. The pastor called him into the office and dismissed him from his duties. He asked him to leave since he was not willing to seek further help outside the church. Without hesitation, this man left that church and went to the church down the road. When the pastor found out where he went, he called the pastor of the church he now attended. The new pastor did not care about the problem of discipline; he just wanted the warm body in the church. With this kind of cooperation between churches, how will anyone find help? This is the kind of man Jesus said to count as a heathen or publican. This means he needs to be evangelized. He needs to confess his sins, repent, and be saved. He has missed the mark and morally sinned against God and the church. Is he redeemable? Yes, but he must be willing to come under discipline of the Word of God by the church.

It's sad when you actually feel like you need to do a background check on the people that come to church. I often wished for a database we can refer to when someone obnoxious and rebellious comes into our church. I love it when I see the stable sheep recognize that this is not what they have learned since they are respectful and careful not to hurt others. When the sheep know the Word or the voice of the Master, they will not stand for someone coming in and bullying them into rebellion or disrespect of the pastors and leadership. (II Timothy 3:1-7 KJV)

Please Pray This Aloud

Father, you have seen the times that I have been sadly disappointed and became bitter over the way people have treated me. I have tried in myself to hide the fact that I was in pain over the words they spoke against me and their actions toward me. I realize in myself that I cannot fix all the things that have happened. I have been angry at them. I have lashed out, and I have isolated myself from the sheep. Please forgive me for my response to the people of God. I was wrong for the way I have acted toward them. I have neglected them due to the hurt I have felt in my heart concerning those that speak against me. I feel that they do not love or appreciate what I do for the church. They love my husband and respect him, but not me. Please help me to love them even when I do not receive love in return. I want my heart to be pure before you, Lord. I want to live in peace with my church family.

Lord, please give me the strength to do what is right and cover the sin toward me with your great love, since your love covers a multitude of sins. Wash over me with your Agape love so that I will be healed of all sheep bites. Heal even the very look and words that they spoke. I depend upon your love to wash me clean and make me whole, and as you make me whole I can again respond with the love and devotion that I want to have toward the sheep. Jesus, you died for the people that we minister to, and I want to love them like you love them.

I let go of all bitterness of my soul. I refuse to allow my soul to talk to me and stir up any ungodly emotions about the people. I let go of all offenses, every look, every misunderstanding. I let go of the false accusations against me. I let go of injustices I have experienced. I bring all this pain to the foot of the cross. I lay them before you Lord Jesus, the one that understands my pain.

Give me the ability to minister your unfailing love to the precious people of God. I forgive them, and I free them from any debt they may owe me. I free them from any false expectations I have placed on them, and I release myself from all false expectations they have been concerning me.

Please give me new opportunities to minister to the church, in any way you want me to be used for the kingdom. Thank you for forgiving me and cleansing me by the Word of God. Amen

Chapter 10

Your Reputation Precedes You!

It is amazing what people think they know about you, even if they have never met you before. Many times I have been introduced in a public place or at church, when suddenly, they do a double take and ask my name again, only to give a look that I cannot explain and I dare not ask about. I am too sensitive to hear all the stories they have heard about me through the grapevine. I am dumbfounded by the amount of hearsay about a pastor or his wife. I've been complimented and I've been insulted, all by people who just met me! They witlessly say something that they thought might be a spiritual observation concerning me, but in the process, show little tact and no intelligence. It's enough to make you not want to venture out of your circle of influence.

Consider the Source

I cannot imagine how some of the celebrity pastors must feel when they are approached by someone who does not care for their soul but yet needs to express how they feel. No wonder these big name evangelists have body guards and fencing erected in their meetings! Girls, this may sound cruel, and perhaps it is, but people sometimes do not think before they engage their mouth. Once I found myself in an uncomfortable position at a very large Christian conference. We were going out the side door reserved for preachers and ministries only. How this particular woman got there was beyond me, but some people just have a way of worming into places they don't belong. She saw me and yelled my name. I turned to greet her and the next words out of her mouth were criticism of me. Of course, wouldn't you know I was standing with a well-known evangelical team. "Pastor Sandy, you have changed," she said. "I remembered you as very harsh and . . . ." she trailed off with more, but I could not move fast enough to get out of the sound of her voice and her insults. I was angry at her ignorance and disgusted that she would say it in front of complete strangers. However, I was not devastated since I considered the source. Yes, I had to go home and repent all over again.

Many times we have to leave it with, "consider the source." We cannot be held responsible for everything that people will say about us, and we do not have to take it into our heart either. It's not worth our time, girls! I always try to evaluate if what they said was worthy to consider for change, or whether it's just a ploy of the devil to throw me off track.

Leg of Toyne, Anyone?

At times my name is brought up at the dinner table with "Oh, that Pastor Sandy..." I know when my name has been used in a derogatory manner since I have great discernment. It does not take a rocket scientist to notice the look on the face of the children or teens after this has happened. They never look at me in the same way, especially when you have become part of the menu. It is so disappointing to realize that some people have such lack of respect or the fear of God that they speak against his anointed pastors and shepherds. I have seen many older teens walk out of the church without looking back because the parents talked about the leaders in an accusatory manner.

Did the parents not realize when they spoke those hurtful angry words in front of the children that even though they may not understand the words, they do understand the halo (body) language, the raising of the voice, the hand movement, the angry faces and the names used? If the child has been raised in the church and has known the pastor for a long period of time, they will know if the trouble has anything to do with them. The thing I know to do in this situation is to firmly confront the people with grace, but love the child, even if they are unfriendly toward you. The parents may change their mind since they were "letting off steam," but the child may be confused. Keep loving and treating those children as before, and they will see for themselves that you are a loving and approachable person.

Give Honor to Where Honor is Due

People have heard another person's story or opinion of you, whether it be bad or good. Let's talk about the good first. Sometimes people come to me for help because I helped a friend of theirs. That person talked me up so much that I did not know they were talking about me. "Go to Pastor Sandy, she will do you good. She helped me, and I know she will minister to you as well." This is wonderful to hear when people give credit where credit is due. Hearing these types of words gives honor to the woman of God and encourages you to do more. I believe when I start hearing praise like that, it is time to give back the evening sacrifice of praise to the Lord and let Him know that it is only by His strength and wisdom we can do anything. The people may want to thank us for what we do for them and that is all right, but we need to keep pointing to Jesus. (Ps. 141:2 KJV)

The Negative Side

Girls, now let us get into the negative side of our reputation. At any given time, we may have to take part of a confrontation of a church member. They may need some type of church discipline that you have to be involved in as part of the pastoral staff duties. I do not like confrontation. I have miserably failed at some and have passed on the others. It takes great strength to be able to do this without getting all stirred up inside. Ideally, the person should come in and discuss what is wrong and submit to correction, rebuke, reproof, and then repent over the sin. This sounds easy enough until they start arguing with you and letting you know all your faults. Nobody said I was perfect, but I am trying my best to be a good pastor's wife or pastor. This is not about me, but it is about their sin or mistake. If this could be kept on track, what a happy world pastors would live in, but it certainly is not reality.

By the time this type of confrontation is over, you don't know who the sinner is and what really happened. Girls, has this ever happened to you before? They saw you coming and they did not want the focus on themselves and their own problem, so instead they turned the tables on you or your husband. By the time they got through with you, you did not know if you were even called to preach. They got mad and left the church, but not before telling you off and then spreading half-truths or lies about you around town.

If this is not bad enough, when others meet you at church or socially, they already have an opinion formed about you. You did not deserve it, but they have judged you on another person's opinion about you and they will not accept you as a spiritual leader. This is foolishness since the Bible instructs us not to believe one until we have heard the other side. I have seen children inside the church look at me with contempt or fear, and I wondered who was talking about me in such a derogatory way that even the children prejudged me. I do believe parents have much to answer for when they speak negatively and disrespectfully of the spiritual authorities God has placed over them. When this happens to me, I try to not let it bother me too much. Sometimes it does because they do not have respect and they say what they have heard about me. I try to forgive them for speaking ignorantly and then do my best to welcome them into the church. At this stage only God can change their mind about me by my actions. They will watch, and it may take awhile, but I have to be myself and be steady in what I believe. I am still a leader, and I have to act like one. I do not have much time to go into a corner and lick my wounds. If we are honest and sincerely love the people, that Agape love will come to the top and prove the instigators wrong. We have to walk in God's love.

I noticed one day in church that someone quoted something I said, but I did not recognize the words. I would never say such a thing. Nevertheless, a beneficial lesson I learned is that the people hear with their own ears and interpret what we say by their own values and understanding. No wonder some people get mad at the pastors. Their understanding is being filtered through faulty hearing and receiving. That can be scary for the pastors.

Don't Blame Me . . .

I have had people use me as a weapon to scare their children into obeying them. When I hear this, I shudder, but I also am bold enough to gently correct them. I let them know that I do not want the children to be afraid of me. We all keep the rules of conduct in a church. Do not blame Pastor Sandy for being the tyrant of the church that hides in corners just waiting to catch a kid in some mischievous act of vandalism. I want to be able to love on the kids no matter what age they are and not have them run and hide or sneak around thinking that the hammer is coming down on them. Girls, do not let the parents get away with this. Some day the children will grow up and marry. You want them to be inside the church with their own families. This is very rewarding for pastors.

Whatever the case may be, when people talk about you in a negative way, the first thing we must do is to forgive them. Make a covenant with the Lord that the information you know about the person will not be made public knowledge just because the person maligns you. If they decide to do this, then there is a judgment they will have to face with the Lord. You wish they would come back to the church and repent to you for making accusations against you falsely, but sometimes that does not happen. Therefore, again, we must take the high road and forgive them.

I heard a pastor's wife say "we were just ready to mark them," when they left the church. Numerous times we have the ability and the knowledge to bring damage to the slanderer. As pastors, we must be careful to follow the instructions in the Word of God. Paul did not hesitate to mark those who cause division and name those who deserted him or cause him great distress in the ministry. We must be wise and realize it is better to say nothing. When I was younger, I thought I had to explain my side of the story and at times, this is unavoidable. Really, the person who has prejudged you will have to discern by your fruit and your track record. This can be a hard place to be in. You want everyone to think well of you as a leader, but you do not know what lies are being said about you. I do much praying in the Spirit at a time like this when I cannot defend myself. I will have to stay quiet before people and cry out to God in my prayer closet. He knows the truth and the truth will eventually come to the surface and set us free. When we try to justify ourselves, we sound guilty. We can dig ourselves a hole and it is hard to climb out. Stay sweet and pray often that God can lift this attack off you and change the other person who is trying to damage your reputation. Remember the devil is the accuser of the brethren so use your spiritual weapons, not carnal weapons which cause more confusion and strife.

The Lord Fights Our Battles

The account of David and Shimei is a great example of the Lord fighting our battle for us if we keep quiet. Many times we fail since we feel as if we have to fight so that someone will understand and agree with us. King David's son Absalom turned against his father. David had to run for his life. He escaped with his family and his mighty men. One lone man, he must have had a death wish to throw rocks and curses at David. Shimei said the Lord was the one that turned against David and he deserved everything that was happening to him. Ahishai, a mighty man in the king's army, could take him out in a moment, but asked before he killed the man. David said "no, do not kill him maybe the Lord will look at my affliction, and he will give me good for what he is lying about." (II Samuel 16: 5-13; Ps. 37 KJV)

Forgive and Release

The best and most effective weapon we have is to forgive and release. If you have not caused this attack on your character, wait on God. If you did something to offend them and did not take care of it, go to them and ask forgiveness. If they forgive you, you have gained a friend; if not, at least you did your part. Go in peace and stay sweet. Accept the fact that not everybody will like us. Just because they are in the church does not mean they are saved or that they want to follow the guidelines set out in the Bible. They may not want to submit, and they may not want to be told what to do. They may not want a pastor or shepherd. They may just want to go to church.

If you teach your people how to respond to someone who is talking or maligning their leaders, they will not listen to an accusation against an elder. They most likely can gently reprove the person for speaking that way against you. If we live in peace, then the Lord will fight our battles. It is surprising, though, the things we never hear that our faithful people say to the others who spoke disrespectfully of us. You would be proud of the way they stick up for you and admire you, in spite of your own failures and shortcomings. All I know is that I do not want to know the times someone stuck up for me when others were talking about me. I am too sensitive to hear everything that people have observed and disliked about me. Had I heard all these things, I would never get behind the pulpit to preach, give announcements or even a testimony. God protects us from hearing everything. Thank God for the faithful, caring people who loyally stand with us.

Jay Adams gave some good advice for those dealing with people who want to talk about someone else. He said, "Let them know at the beginning of the conversation that you would be telling the person they were going to talk about the content of the discussion." This can save untold words and sin when we are blunt about this. The Bible says if you have ought against another, you are to go to him or her. It did not tell you to voice it around the church. Girls, when we can properly follow through with this principle of resolving gossip in our church, we will save ourselves untold hours of stress and live in peace. Practice these yourselves, pastor's wives, and teach it on a regular basis. It will come back to you press down, shaken together, and running over shall men give back to you. If you teach Scriptures, the people will follow what you do. They learn more when you lead by example and the Lord will reward you openly for your willingness to practice godly character. [29]

Shepherding God's Flock; Jay E. Adams, Chapter XII House Calling page 92

Let's Pray

Dear Jesus, there have been times that I felt so misjudged. I felt as if I lived in a glass house or that I was under the microscope. People have judged me before they even got to know me. I felt like they have not given me a chance. They do not even like me. Lord, you put us in this church for a time and a season. I know I cannot run from this and I cannot stay hurt. But, Father God, this really hurts me. I am so lonely. I feel like it's me against the people. I do not want to feel like this. Please come and bring peace to my mind and my emotions. Lord, teach me how to make this right. I know I had something to do with this whole quarrel. Help me to humble myself before you. Help me to go to those I have intentionally or unintentionally hurt. Give me the courage to do my part to make things right. I pray that you will give me peace and please help me to make friends; I do not want to live like this. Let me be an example to the people. I pray as I make this humble effort that you would also give courage to those who also need to make peace with me. Please let me love the people with your Agape love, and I pray that the people will see a change in me and give me another chance to love them with your unconditional love. Amen

Chapter 11

Mom's Prayers

Reverend Dolly

One of the greatest role models I have in my life when it comes to prayer is my 84-year old mother, Dolly Nelson. She has been an inspiration to me over the years. She loved to pray when I was a child, although I was not always appreciative. She would rise early to read the Bible and pray before the kids awoke for school. Every morning, when I got up at 6:00 am, Mom already had her prayer time in and her devotions done. When you are young you take that sort of discipline and devotion for granted.

Throughout my life, I have enjoyed times of prayer. As a teen I would pray at length, seeking God on how I should live my life for Him. As a new mother, I continued with fervency when the children were young. I did not realize how intense the prayers would become when my babies grew into the teenagers. I could always depend on my mom to support my family in prayer. There was something so special about calling Mom to say "could you pray for . . ?" Even with miles between us, if she did not hear from me, she would be calling to see what was going on in our life. Never did she give a judgment, or opinion, and she never ever said, "This is the last time I am praying for your family!"

Our children now have families of their own and spend time praying for their own children. Now they call me like I have always called my mom asking for prayer. Some things never change. Mom never forgets to ask about the kids and grandkids, and often she says that she has been praying for them. I still call her and ask her to pray for whatever is going on at the time. My mom, Reverend Dolly, retired from the pastoral office, but she has never once thought of retiring from making a ministry of prayer and intercession for others. She has faithfully prayed for all of her children and friends through some very rough situations. She is not in the best of health at times, but it has never stopped her from praying. I know her last breath will be some type of communing with God for others.

I thank God that when she retired, she did not give up on prayer. Mom is a great example to all aging men and women who feel they are not useful, especially those who have been struck with illness or lived through death of their spouse. They can still pray and believe God for the answer. Often times when sleep does not come easily to Mom, I know she will be praying for those she loves. She has seen and heard many answered prayers over the years. Oh, to have a group of men and women who fought the battles of life upon their knees in prayer and found the answers in the Word of God! These are the people I want on my team when I am going through hard times: people who realize that Jesus is just a prayer away and to never give up.

When my mom would come and stay with me, I would often check on her before I would go to bed. I would pause at the closed door, listening to see if I would hear her in prayer since I did not want to disturb her. Many times I would hear her as she was halfway through the kids, or sometimes she would pray for those who were in the hardest battle at the time. Nonetheless, she would be praying for each one of her children.

When Mom goes home to be with the Lord, I often wonder who will take her place. Will someone else rise up? Will someone else build themselves a watchtower, so they can see what is happening in their families in order to pray? I truly hope our family will rise and seek the Lord for their children and grandchildren as Reverend Dolly has all these years. When she goes, her absence will be noticed and people will wonder, who shall I call now for prayer? Who will care for my soul as much as dear old Reverend Dolly did?

My husband Dennis has the very same habit that my mother does. When he wakes up, he pours a cup of coffee, and with his Bible laid out on the kitchen table, he spends his quiet time with the Lord. You can hear him pray wherever he is around the house. He prays while he is doing chores or working outdoors— he even prays in the shower! Rarely have I not heard him pray and sing praises to His Lord God throughout each day.

Dennis and I have a rule in our house: whoever gets up first makes the coffee, but we do not wake the other. We both like to quietly pray and watch the sun rise and its light fill the house. I do not like to have lights on, and he does not like the TV on, so over the years we have observed each other's way of having that special time with the Lord.

Less Than 15 Minutes a Day

Fact:

- 80% of pastors spend under 15 minutes a day in prayer.[30]

I read a survey where most pastors spend less than fifteen minutes per day in prayer. Now that is down right scary! No wonder men and women are failing in the pastoral office! How can you cope with this job that is very time consuming, truly full of stress, and, at times, heartache? We are there when a loved one goes home to be with the Lord. We are there when they have to put their elderly parents in nursing homes. We are there when someone is diagnosed with a terminal illness. We are there when the children are born. We are there when something happens to one of those children. We are there when they lose their job and have to move away or give up their home. We are there in the court system sitting through someone's trial and sentencing. We are there to officiate at the wedding, and, sad to say, see them end in divorce. We are there through all of the counseling, and still see that it did not make a difference, as they walk away from the marriage. We are there to watch them struggle financially and be fearful for the future. We are there when they have family problems and there is no peace. We are there when their child has made a terrible mistake in judgment and must pay the consequences. We are there in almost every part of a member's life *if they will allow us to be*. We see and feel their heartache and pain. It is not easy to give instruction from the Word of God, which they simply cannot or will not grasp. It is hard when they do not believe what is true but choose to go their own way. The list is endless but there is hope. Prayer is the hope. If a pastoral unit does not pray at these times of distress, they will eventually fail. We must find that altar of prayer so you can regain your strength. This is what Paul said in II Corinthians 11: 28: (KJV) The word care means: solicitude, anxiety, concern. Paul was responsible for the operation of all the churches, programs etc and we as pastors are as well. *"Beside those things that are without, that which cometh upon me daily, the care of all the churches. . ."*

Girls, I do not want to only paint a gloomy picture. I just want you to be aware of what could happen. Good things can and do happen as well. I get so excited when I see that someone finds Jesus as their Lord and Savior. At that time the angels rejoice in heaven, and we rejoice on earth. When people have found their hope in the Lord, they have seen the hand of God work in their lives and have had prayers answered. The matters were impossible to be answered by man, but God arrived and brought miracles. We have seen many healings and miracles: physical, financial, and in the families. We have watched God perform His Word just like the Bible states. I have seen the parents pray for the prodigal to come home, and they did. We rejoiced over the lost sheep found. We have the privilege to officiate at weddings, where the bride and groom have established the tradition to raise their family in the church.

We delight to watch the young moms and dads come in, one carrying a child and the other a diaper bag. I have the awesome pleasure of taking the new little one up to the altar and introducing them to the congregation. I feel like Mufasa on *The Lion King* when he goes to the highest mountain and presents little Simba to the people. I know I do not have to remind you how important the little ones are to Jesus. (St .Mark 10:14 KJV) Soon they will lead the people. The babes are introduced to the ones who have been closest to mom and dad. I let them know that this is the man, Pastor Dennis, who has been preaching to them for the last nine months, and now they get to meet him. I hold them high in the air so all can rejoice with the parents that a new member has arrived at Cornerstone Family Church and they are very welcome. We dedicate those little ones and promise we will do whatever we can to see that they know God. We get to watch the little ones grow into toddlers (when they actually think they own the church!) Since they have been with us as infants, I have some that do not want to leave on Sunday or Wednesday. Crying loudly and hanging onto the door, they beg to stay with their friends. We have to stoop down and say that it's time to go home and we'll see them again soon. We get to watch all of them grow and graduate from one class to another. I love to watch the little ones become teens who still love church. Just recently, our daughter went on a vacation and other situations arose where our grandchildren were not able to attend church. My grandson Zach confronted his mom, "What's up with you? Why can't we go to church?" It is our delight to be able to counsel those going off to college and getting married. They are so full of life and hope, and it makes me smile. I am so proud of them. I get excited when others step up and want to help in anyway they can. We have the privilege of being with the congregation through all of the triumphs and accomplishments of life.

No Substitutes for Prayer!

In all the pastoral work that we do and experience, we need to pray. There cannot be anything else to replace it. Jesus was our example. *When you pray….*
(Matt. 6: 5 KJV)

- When he began his ministry, he fasted for forty days and nights.
  (Matthew 4) Jesus found the power for ministry in that time of prayer.
- Jesus became popular because of the miracles; the people pressed him from every side. They followed him everywhere not allowing him to rest because of their great need. He found that place to pray. Prayer will keep us humble as we bend our

knee to God the creator of heaven and earth. Jesus knew the power did not come from any man but from God. (Mark 1:35, 6:46-47, Lu. 5:15, 16,)

- When John the Baptist was beheaded, Jesus found a place to pray. Matthew 14 in our time of grief; prayer is the place we need to go and find our comfort. We can take comfort in many things, but in Father's presence is fullness of joy.
- When Jesus performed miracles and healings, and people pressed him for more, he found a place to pray. Matt. 15:22 Jesus remembered the miracle working power was not in himself, for he had laid it all aside, and walked in the power of the Spirit, Luke 4:18.
- When the religious leaders of the day persecuted Jesus and wanted to kill him, he found a place to pray. Our protection is through the power of the armor of Christ and applied with prayer. Eph. 6
- When his disciples and family did not understand his ministry and the words he spoke, he found a place to pray. Our example is Jesus. Many times family and friends do not understand that we have to take time to pray and study the Word. They go to play and we have to stay at home and pray. Girls, this is only a part of the price of ministry. Jesus shows us how to pay that price in prayer.
- When it was the time of Jesus' betrayal, he was found in the Garden of Gethsemane praying. One of the most terrible times of ministry is the time nobody will stand with you. At times you feel like the loneliest person in the world and yet in that prayer time, you hear the voice of God saying well done thou good and faithful servant. (Luke 22:41-42 KJV)
- Even on the cross Jesus prayed. It was only a few brief words that Jesus spoke through lips of agony. However, in those words, volumes of thought were given; forgiving his murderers, forgiving a thief, speaking to the Father, proclaiming the completion of the work. He prayed in the most disadvantaged time of any persons' life. The love of God flowed from his holy lips as he spoke these words. This

is what we will hear too in the deepest of agonies. (Luke 23: 34 KJV)

The Need Was Great

We may have a time when we are so busy with the people that we do not take proper time to pray. I see in these incidents that indeed Jesus went away by himself or with his team of disciples to pray. The need was great. Hopeless cases, desperate people, the sick, diseased, demonized, were brought to him.

There were four times in the Gospel of Mark when Jesus found a place to pray. It does not matter how large your church is; there will be people who will want more time than you can give. Nevertheless, we need to be able to say no, so that we may keep our boundaries, set our priorities, and find time to pray. Intrusions and issues will arise in the church when we wished we would have been able to pray first. Sometimes we just say, "We cannot decide now. We have to pray about it." The need of the people will pull on us as it did Jesus. He was moved with compassion, and we must do the same.

The Garden Prayers

The religious leaders had tried to trick him. They lied about him. They accused him of many things. Jesus prayed in the Garden of Gethsemane, "not my will but thine be done." He went through that lonesome time when no one stayed awake with him to pray. The battle was raging. He sweat great drops of blood in this battle of his will and the Fathers.

As pastors, we may end up in a battle, although many times our battle is not unto death. We may get off course in what God has asked us to do. We may be facing terrible persecution and trials inside the church. This may be your worst hour of decision where you will have to say like Jesus did, "Not my will, but, Fathers, yours be done." Do not make that major decision in haste and without proper prayer. Jesus took time to wrestle with his flesh and to again hear the plan of God, and so must we. At our worst moments, we need to ask for the Holy Spirit to reveal 'the plan' again to us. What was the original plan? Have you fulfilled it? We asked others to pray with us, but soon they grew weary just as the disciples did. When all fall asleep around us, we must still pray. The answer will come if only we pray, although it helps to have that spirit of unity working amid the turmoil.

Jesus taught his disciples to pray, because it was very important to him that they knew how to pray. He set the standard of how and when to pray. He knew that there would be times when without prayer, they would not be able to stand in the time of tribulation and trials. It comes to all of us. How you will stand if you do not pray? What will you go to for your comfort? How far will you run or isolate yourself from the troubles that knock at your door, or at the church?

Go back to your roots, those moments that you spent much time in prayer, just you and the Lord. When you find the altar of prayer, He will never disappoint you.

Girls, Please Pray with Me

Lord, I have allowed myself to run on empty many times, and my last resort was prayer when I was faced with a crisis. I was not in touch with you; I could not hear my master's voice. It should have been easy to hear you, but I so often ignored your promptings to come for sweet fellowship of prayer. I have gone away from prayer because of the pull of the people and the business of my life. Now it is as if I, myself have been weighed in a balance and found wanting.

There are times I have judged you as not listening to me so I left prayer. I left communicating with you. I was discouraged and felt that you did not love me because certain vital prayers were not answered according to how I thought they should be. So I pulled away from you. I felt that you embarrassed me by not answering the prayers I publically proclaimed. It became easier to stay busy in the church; I felt that I had accomplished something to replace the disappointment in my soul.

Please forgive me for not turning to you first to pray, I was wrong for shutting you out of my life or using prayer only as a tool and not having a relationship with you. Teach me to pray, to humble myself, and communicate with you. Forgive me for trying to rule as a god. Forgive my thought that all my prayers need to be answered according to my will and demand, and not according to Your great plan. Please forgive me for my rebellion and indolence.

I want to be a good example to my family and to my church. Please give me the strength to change my habit of praying on the run and not communicating directly to you. Give me a heart to pray like I use to before discouragement set in. I now set myself to seek your face. Thank you, Lord for hearing me when I pray. Amen

Chapter 12

Hey Pastor, You Need a Pastor!

Facts:

- 70% of pastors constantly fight depression.
- 50% of pastors are so discouraged that they would leave the ministry if they could, but they have no other way of making a living
- 61% of pastors admit that they "have few close friends."[31]

It can be very lonely when you do not have a support system you can rely upon when needed. The Assemblies of God evidently understood this principle when forming monthly district counsel meetings for their pastors. Certainly, at times it seemed inconvenient for us to travel to one of the churches involved and spend our whole day with other pastors. If we were going through a particularly rough battle, it was certainly more difficult to muster up courage and put on a happy face. We may have griped and complained to each other about going, but once we got there, we would find encouragement. There was an understanding between the pastors and their wives. We knew what the other was going through since we were there ourselves. Though it may have been a 'business meeting,' it was a time of fellowship and preaching.

At this time in our lives we were living in rural Iowa, where most towns were less than 10,000 in population. The churches were all about the same size with the same struggles. Very few pastors had been in the same church for many years. Most of us were new to the pastoral ministry. We were young, filled with enthusiasm and energy. Some of us would come willingly to these meetings. Others would come but not participate, since they were only there out of obligation. It was an agreement with the Assemblies of God organization that you would attend the monthly meetings. Your district presbyter would call you to make sure you knew the time and the place of the meeting. Each month a different church would host the meeting. The various churches really liked this since they would be able to show off the excellent cooks they had in their church.

I especially remember our dear "Pie Lady" named Marie. She would set this event in order and would bake up a storm. She taught me how to not only put a banquet together that was fit for a king, but to enjoy it as well. Marie was so full of the love of God that it oozed out of her. Her love was serving people, and she made the best food. She loved to see the smile on their face when they would take the first bite. She taught me how to make the most excellent Coconut Cream Pie and Apple Cobbler. In fact, I still make her Apple Cobbler for our son's birthday.

These times were invaluable for us personally; we gleaned much information from the ministers that came to speak to us. They would preach messages that were relevant for the young preachers and their wives. The messages would encourage us and keep us going for another month. We would exchange stories with each other and learn about different programs they were initiating in the church. Each month we would meet and the same ministers would come. We started to form meaningful relationships with them. It was a wonderful time to sit around a table in a church fellowship hall and have times of sharing our work with a fellow minister couple.

We have all since moved on to other ministries. Some have left the pastoral call completely. I look back over that time in a new pastorate, and I know that this was one of the elements that kept us in that Assembly of God church for eleven years.

You Need A Pastor

Younger couples in ministry (and by "younger" I'm referring to experience, not age) must realize that they are in need of a pastor in the same way that a congregation needs a shepherd. Yes, some belong to an organization, but many times these organizations do not have an open door policy. We belonged to and supported a certain organization only by name. It was a status symbol, but there was no one within that organization who we could actually could go to and bounce ideas off of. We did not have a representative close by us, so we would travel once a year to be part of the large group. Sometimes, we would have impersonal phone calls, but all those things did was make us feel as though we were outsiders.

Sometimes a preacher just needs another preacher friend who can understand what he is actually going through. Many times we felt that if we had a problem it had better be a substantial one to justify wasting the time of a busy presbyter. After all, he had his own church to deal with.

I was glad when we went back to having someone close by. It makes life easier when we are going through a hard spot in the road to be able to contact a pastoral couple. It is invaluable to meet somewhere for dinner and then return refreshed because they listened, offered suggestions, and prayed with us and for us. Most times all we really need is someone to listen to us and understand the weight of the ministry, since they carry it as well.

We now have about five couples we can call on within a one-hundred mile radius. One couple we meet with on a regular basis. Neither of us has church on Sunday evening so we meet for a movie and dinner. We have talked in restaurants until they close the doors! We try to solve all the worlds' problems and listen to each others sermons for the day. We share our hopes, dreams and disappointments. We trade godly advice with each other. I treasure those times. There is no chief, and we come on common ground. We are pastors who need to be around others with like precious faith. There are always times of laughter. Some times there is sadness as we grieve with each other over the loss of a precious member of the flock.

I have friends that if I call and say I need to meet with them, they know it is serious and will drop whatever they can to meet us halfway. We have taken them out on our pontoon and just sat in the middle of the water so we could be alone and talk about the things that are troubling each others' hearts. It is plain and simple. We are on the same level. No one tries to be an expert on the subject. We listen and are concerned for our brother or sister in the Lord. These times where we are able to say what we need to say, without judgment or criticism, but with a heart full of empathy instead, this is invaluable to us as pastors.

God has certainly blessed us. If we did not have a support group to lean on, we would feel like we are out here all alone. That's exactly what the devil wants you to believe, but it is not true. There are those who would love to have a friendship like we have with our handful of pastors. In order to have this Proverbs 24 says, "A man that hath friends must shew himself friendly." (KJV) This is certainly true; we must work at being friends. Sometimes we reach out a hand of friendship, but it becomes one-sided. Perhaps they do not trust or think they need any fellowship. In any case, we are no worse off because at least we have tried.

Pastors of a Different House

There was a time, and it still exists today, where church organizations are not 'thrilled' with you fellowshipping outside the confines of your own organization. We do not agree with that philosophy. We feel like others may have something to offer in the way of truth and fellowship. Many times we have gone to various church meetings held by the Independent Churches, Word Pastors, and Denominational Churches. We cannot find anything in the Word of God that tells us to stay away from those who are not in a certain organization. (Romans 14:4)

Even though Paul had a work of his own, he would agree to certain stipulations of the Scriptures and travel to Jerusalem to be part of the Church Council of the Apostles.

Paul corrected those who would try to bring separation by saying "I am of Appollos, I am of Peter, I am of Paul" He tried to bring unity and understanding by instructing that "some plant the seed, some water, but God gives the increase." We all have a part to play. (I Cor. 1:12; I Cor. 3 KJV)

I think what hurts pastors is how the people wander and compare pastor to pastor. It can cause insecurities to rise within us, especially if our people are not loyal. I can say for myself, "I want to plant the seed, see them get saved; I want to water their garden with the refreshing of the Holy Spirit and the Word of God. And I want them to stay in my church." That's how I feel, and I think most pastors feel the same way. Yes, it is selfish and maybe immature, but I want the reward for the fields I have labored in. "Behold, how good and how pleasant it is for brethren to dwell together in unity! 2. It is like the precious ointment upon the head, that ran down upon the beard, even Aaron's beard: that went down to the skirts of his garments." (Psalms 133: 1-2 KJV)

Unity speaks volumes to the Lord and to the world. The oil that saturated Aaron at his anointing had a strong aromatic fragrance which penetrated the skin. It represents the oil of the Holy Spirit and it brings acknowledgement to us and the people when they catch the scent of the anointing. It reminds us of the responsibility we have to the whole body of Christ. We are not an island to ourselves, even though we may be so busy that we forget we have other brothers and sisters who carry the same call. Who are we to not recognize the same call on someone other than yourself or your organization? "As the dew of Hermon, and as the dew that descended upon the mountains of Zion: for there the Lord commanded the blessing, even life for evermore." (Ps.133: 3 KJV) The dew that fell again saturated the area, and all the people were affected by the refreshing dew. It was a reminder that this anointing comes from a higher source than us.

I had the opportunity to have lunch with the pastor's wife of a large church in the area. I was so pleased to hear her story of how they came into the ministry and the different programs that they have established in the community. She was so excited about her call to the Church. There was nothing different about her from the other pastor's wife I had invited to lunch, when it came to the hopes and dreams they shared. They were both equally busy about the work of the ministry. One had a large church, the other a small church. Both women were fulfilled and happy working to the good of the church. The only difference I heard was that the larger church had more people to help carry the load, although I will have to say the larger church pastors had many more responsibilities than just pastoring. In the smaller church, the pastors worked very hard between secular jobs and ministry.

Is Anybody Out There? I Will Be at the Pier at 12:00 Noon

Did you watch the movie *I am Legend?* Each day the main character would radio broadcast that he would be in a specific location at a specific time, just in case there was anyone else just like him out there. He was desperate to be with his own kind.

That scene makes me think of the pastors who really do not have anyone around them. I do not know if they do not want to go through the hassle of meeting new pastors, or if they do not want to have to explain themselves to other pastors. But girls, I do know if you will take a chance in making new friends, they will invite you into their circle.

I know firsthand how sweet the fellowship can be to have pastors as your friends, confidants, and prayer partners. One day, I decided that I wanted to expand my horizon. I know there are pastors' wives who are so busy with church, secular jobs, and family, that they do not have much time for themselves, let alone friendships. These women have poured all of their energies into keeping up with what they have to do day by day. They have no time to do a breakfast or lunch with a friend. Yet, I still try to make contact with them, letting them know that they still need to take those breaks and that I would love to take them out for lunch.

Some pastor's wives do not give me the time of day. They ignore my letters, emails, or phone calls. Okay, I get it. They do not need any other friendships, which is fine. Yet when she looks back over all her hard work and sacrifice, will she have any pastoral friends that she can call on? Girls, do you realize that most pastors go through the same issues that others do? It is just a matter of time before trouble, heartache and disappointment, comes knocking at your door. It has nothing to do with pride, does it? Maybe your church is going through a difficult time, and you do not want to share it because you do not want anyone to judge you as being a 'bad' pastor. That is highly unlikely, since we have experienced almost everything you can think of in our long term as pastors.

I can understand how you may feel. Some pastors seem to have the answer for everything. We certainly do not need that. We need someone to listen to and understand us. So many times when we have gotten together with pastors, things became very competitive. This will not help. The pastor who was trying to build relationship found they could not get a word in to the one-sided conversation. I have been in that group. It sure seemed like all they wanted to do was talk or boast about themselves. Folks like that are either very selfish or very insecure. This is frustrating for a pastoral couple and will not help to build a lasting relationship. No wonder pastors are turned off and will not enter into any type of setting with the other pastors who only want to talk about themselves.

I like to hear what other people are doing, so that I can get new ideas. If you allow the other to talk awhile, you can see where their heart is. They need fellowship. Some don't think they do until they finally socialize with other pastors and realize they had a good time in doing so!

I hate to say it, but I think some people love to be alone in their little kingdom. They do not care how large or small it is, just as long as they are king. They are the ones that other people look to. There is a rush in having a following, and a people who do not question your authority. They just love you. That may be part of the ministry, but isolation is not the answer.

Others think they are the only ones that are doing it right, even if you only have a handful of people. In larger churches, there is a nucleus of other leaders in your church, and you may be completely satisfied with who is on your staff and how you relate to them. This is fine until you feel the crunch of being the senior pastor, and you suddenly you realize that you do not have anyone to whom you can confide. I know it may seem hard for you to go down to a pastor who has only a tithe of what you pastor. You may feel you couldn't possibly share anything in common. But that smaller church pastor still has wisdom and has been through much of the same. If you are not comfortable with that, find a pastor of your same caliber and calling. Make friends with them so you can have those times of fellowship. To become isolated is not a good thing. When that happens, who will correct you if you get off center with a doctrine?

Who are you accountable to? Who will stop you from destroying the church by some of your off-the- wall decisions or anger? There is a reason why we need to have those with the same qualifications and calling around about us. It is to safeguard the church and to keep us from becoming a tyrant. Remember this is not your kingdom, it belongs to God; Jesus shed his blood and gave up his life for the church.

I'm Too Busy for My Spiritual Parents

I have seen young men and women set out for the pastorate and you could not tell them anything. They have a direct line to God, and they do not need any advice or for anyone to tell them how to operate in their domain. Therefore, you go about your business until they get ready to have time for you, which usually coincides with the time when they hit a snag. There are all sorts of snags in the ministry. You do not need to do it alone. Your spiritual parents have already experienced some of the issues you will no doubt face. They can spare you much heartache and misunderstanding in the church if you will not shut them out. Here are just a few issues you may face in ministry where someone more experienced would be able to help you through.

- Some will dislike your personality: you are too bossy, too laid back, aloof, controlling, not sensitive enough, and so on and so on.
- Church Tradition: This is how we have done it for years and it is not changing now!
- You do it; you have nothing else to do. Clean the church, start a new program, teach a class, etc.
- They do not agree with your doctrines.
- They have pet doctrine and they refuse to budge, even if you can prove incorrect by the Holy Scriptures.
- They do not like how you raise your children.
- They do not like how you care for your husband.
- They do not like how you dress, the car you drive or the house you live in.

- You are the outsider; there is a mentality in the congregation/board against the pastor.
- A woman preacher!
- We like this cozy, run-down church! There is no need for a new building.

I have been that young woman of God who is going to stand by her man. I paid no mind to any sort of adversity. If you would have tried to caution me, I would have thought you were a skeptic, or perhaps an old embittered person who just did not appreciate or recognize what God was going to do with and through us. I would have thought that "this is a new day," and you were just part of an old worn out system of church operations. It is amazing that just after a few years, you will hear the words of that older woman in the ministry and rehearse what she said to you when it came to pass.

You Could Have Sought Counsel

I have found that pastors can get themselves in all sorts of trouble with the church. It could have been prevented by counsel of other pastors before you made it an issue. We in the pastoral office know that at any given moment, someone will have an opinion about something. You may not like it or agree with it, but nonetheless, it could become a large issue, especially if you make a priority to disagree. Some things are better left unsaid. At the very least we should not be so brazened to say, "I am the pastor of this church, and I will let you know what we will do or not do." It will not make a difference in the end. The church really does not belong to the pastor, but to everyone.

I know I have heard the stories of how a board may rule the church to the place where it actually stifles the growth. They have chased away the gifted newcomers who had the ability to bring improvement to an area in the church. But to be fair, I have heard of churches that are so pastor-driven that nothing can be done without his approval, even to the point that only he selects the color of the flowers, etc. Oh please! Let the pastor pray and study, and let the deacons do their ministry. It really works to follow the plan set out in the Word of God. When Pastors have a trust issue, it is hard for them to release authority to anyone, especially if they have been betrayed when they trusted those who eventually deceived them.

Girls, it is important to have trusted pastors in your life to hear what you are doing. You may think it is all right to carry out this type of control and authority. But actually, you are depriving the church and the people from stepping up into positions that they are more than able and called to do. You need someone to look you squarely in the face and gently, but firmly, correct this misconception you have. It is as if you have a death grip on the ministry, and your church will not grow until you release some of the responsibilities to others. Think about this: your church is not growing and here you are so busy and at the same time frustrated because you want the church to grow. What responsibility can you give to another person in your church so you do not have to do it? Instead of complaining of the workload and seeing little progress, try giving ministry opportunities to those who you have around you. Did you ever think that the Lord is trying to teach you to release others into their rightful ministry? Did you ever think that you may be the one who is disobedient, and that is why the church has not prospered as of yet?

Girls, this is why it is so important to take time to know those who labor among you. Make a point to know who they are and how they handle everyday problems of life with family, friends, jobs etc. We are not to lay hands on anyone suddenly. Know who you are authorizing to be in a spiritual position in your church. In addition, from time to time, do an evaluation so if some difficult life situation is occurring in their lives, you can help by working together to resolve it. (I Thess. 5:12; I Tim. 5:22 KJV)

There are people that have great input, and we would be wise to take their advice. God has given us extremely gifted people in the church to come up along a side of us to help us. If you get to know them instead of keeping them at arm's length, you will realize that they too are a gift to the body of Christ. It seems that many times pastors look at people through the eyes of what do they want? On the other hand, are they coming to hurt the church? We may play the twenty-question game and be aloof for some time to see if they are really going to stay with us. The Bible says to know them that work among you.

Another time where pastoral advice comes in handy is when people come to you boasting about what they can do. We have all had people come into our churches like a whirlwind, making all types of boasts and promises of what they can do for the church, and of course, what they do for God. Soon they start pushing their way into the pastor's life, wanting to impress them with how spiritual they are. Right from the get-go they claim God sent them to come to the church and help. Before they are even settled in the church:

- They may make unrealistic and unsolicited promises.
- They may tell you what is wrong with the church and how to fix it.
- They may start asking for positions that are really only for the faithful servants.
- They may try to knock out your leaders to make a place for themselves.
- They may talk way too much about themselves and what God is doing through them.
- They may want to start out on top instead of letting us get to know them by serving.
- If they have anything to give monetarily they may start to try to buy the pastors and people with their gifts.
- They may do too much work, and not pace themselves, so that it looks like they are more active and involved in the church than the pastor or leaders.
- They may have the ability to insinuate without incriminating themselves and put suspicion upon the leaders.
- They seem to show up at the right time to be in on things that do not concern them.
- They may make you feel that you cannot do without them, even though you really do not know them, where they have been or what they have been up to, they are very convincing.
- Always have something to say about the last church they were at and comparing pastor to pastor but you are inevitably fair better than the last one.

These types of people are scary to the pastor's wife, unless they just happen to be a woman who fits right in. You really do not know how they are treating the rest of the women. What makes matters worse is if the women of your church realize that you just got a new friend, and she ends up being your sidekick and shopping pal. She conveniently has nothing to do except serve the pastor's wife. This can be tricky if the person has the wrong motive. What makes it worse is when the husband is elated that you have found a friend who can help meet the needs that he cannot, because he is so engrossed in the church. Even so, you have been set up. Now that "woman friend" is working behind the scenes. One by one she removes all obstacles standing in her way, meaning the other women in the church who have faithfully served you and loved you for who you are, not for what you can do for them.

I remember the time when someone came into our church like that, and at least four faithful friends warned me about this woman. I said "thank you for being concerned about me, and I'll watch and pray." It took me a while to know that things happened behind my back as the person tried to make a place for herself. She wanted to be in ministry and speak into women's lives.

This is a very special place to be able to minister to the women, and it is an honor and privilege (not to mention how fun it can be!) Girls, you know when things go wrong, but you cannot put a finger on it because so much is done "behind your back?" All pastors' wives should have the ability to discern the motives of others. Sometimes it takes time for them to show their hand, and then you realize it. They're not out for the good of the church because they have their own agenda. They want to be exalted and have control. They have very selfish motives which will not promote godliness or love, since they are behind the scenes speaking rebellion, innuendos, etc. into others lives. It is sad that we even have to write such things, but as every pastor's wife knows, it is the truth.

If something like this took place in the beginning of our ministry, I would have been territorial and they would not have stayed very long. However, now that I am older in the Lord, I truly want to help these women. They may not even know how ambitious they really are. They see a call on their own life and want to get there; they seem to think it may be a game of who is better at this, the pastor's wife or the person.

One thing to remember is there will always be people who have more abilities than you, but *you* carry the office of pastor. That gives you clout, not to strong arm others, but to realize that you have a calling and a mandate from the Lord. You really are important in the eyes of the Lord. If you humbly realize that God gave you the church to love and nurture as a pastor's wife, you will not have to worry about someone stealing your thunder or position. You know as well as I do with all the work you are obligated to do that you would enjoy some ladies to help, to make it enjoyable, and to add to your abilities. Let us face it. We do not know how to do it all, but with the help of some loving women of the church, you can learn to do many more things and give duties away to others who are capable without the fear of a takeover. That is sad to write the words "takeover." It sounds like I am either paranoid, or I think I am in a war zone and some terrorist is plotting to take over the USA. This sounds ridiculous and oh, how I wish it was not true, but I have heard many stories over the years and I have also experienced it about 20 years ago. I have been in the ministry a long time, and you do not think anyone would want to take something that belongs to another, especially a church. What's up with that? People who want to steal someone else's church do not know what they are getting into. I truly do not think people know how hard it is to have and grow a church! The everyday difficulties can send the best of pastor's packing, it is hard to hear. Have you ever listened to any of these complaints?

- You did not do . . .
- I know I can do this better than you,
- Why did you not do this?
- The church across town does it this way . . .
- I am leaving, you did not . . . . .
- The church is too small, the church is too big . . .
- Pastor so and so asked me to help him . . . .

There truly is a safe-guard for pastors, if they allow other pastors to be their friends. I know someone always wants to be the leader of the band. I am not necessarily looking for that, just a friend we can call for fun, fellowship, advice, and to just blow off steam or have a prayer meeting.

Chapter 13

And the Survey Says . . .

In writing this book, I thought it would be good to get information concerning what congregations thought of Pastors' wives. I endeavored to get mixed opinions from different churches. I did not realize that some would not want to participate.

I asked several pastors' wives from different locations. To my surprise, some nicely refused me, and when they gave me their reason, I understood. Others would not give me the time of day. They just ignored my requests to have their church participate in this survey. I thought I was a friend to some and would have expected a better answer than to have them totally ignore me.

Some felt they would be opening a can of worms with such questions. I also heard from one who allowed some of her congregation to participate, knowing what may happen. I can understand what these women were feeling, since I asked my own congregation to fill it out, knowing it could back fire on me. I will say even though we have over 200 members in our church, we received only 50-75 completed surveys.

At the onset of this study, I knew I could be offended at some of their answers. It was as if I was asking for people to give their true opinion about me, which now becomes very personal.

When forming this survey, I asked some of my friends who are pastoral wives if they were curious about any particular subjects. Three to four additional pastors wives contributed to the formulation of survey questions. I tried to at least get one hundred surveys, but truthfully, I was surprised with the lack of participation. One person even thought it was a trick to find out what they actually thought of the pastor's wife, as if she recently had trouble with them. Only a handful of people had "an axe to grind." The rest were kind and thoughtful, thinking the best about the person in question. I was surprised how many really did not know the pastor's wife. Others said they would have never wanted them to be the worship leader or to organize an event.

The surveys were sent to Clear Lake, Iowa, and several Wisconsin cities: Oshkosh, Merrill, Sturgeon Bay, and Green Bay. I want to thank all of the pastors for allowing me to plug into their church and glean information from their congregations. Out of these participating churches, I received 100 surveys.

The Real Deal: THE PASTOR'S WIFE SURVEY

Hello, I am writing a thesis on the Pastor's wife, and I am collecting information that will help me write my paper. Could you please fill out this survey and email it back to me or send it to my address? I really appreciate your help. I would like to have this back ASAP.
Thanks, Pastor Sandy Toyne

Please fill in the blank or put a mark by the answers you feel are right, there are no wrong answers.

1. Do you want the pastor wife in each service? Sunday? Midweek? Multiple services on Sunday?

Most people wanted the pastor's wife to be in all of the services. They did not care if there were multiple services or not, they wanted her there. This tells me several things:

1) They do believe the wife should support her husband in whatever he does. It is always good to see her. I've personally have noticed if I do not come to church, people will call me and say they

have been praying for me this week. Some will stop me before or after service and let me know that I was missed the previous Sunday. If there are two consecutive services, I would suggest that she may stay for greeting the people at the second service, but then leave if the day becomes too long for her. Some find a class to teach or office work to do while the second service is in progress. In most churches, there are always questions to be answered, and people look to the pastor's wife for some of the answers.

2) It also lets me know that they do not even consider that she has already heard the sermon at least once before. To them it is important that she is there with husband. I would say if the wife has small children, she should be able to take her children home instead of subjecting them to another Sunday school or Children's Church.

We are experimenting with a Saturday night service, along with the usual Sunday morning service. In this case, I do believe the pastor's wife needs to be there for both services because we still have a whole group of people to minister. We are not the type of pastors who just sit in the front row. When we are needed to pray or give counsel, we are there.

3) Many people wanted the wife to be in the midweek service as well. I also think they should be there with the congregation. What is ironic, midweek is not well attended at times, but they want her there no matter if they attend or not. Do they think we have to be there because it is our job, or for the support of the husband? I know some of the people's jobs do not allow them to come to midweek service. I appreciate their position. I question the member's commitment when they believe I should be in midweek service, but they stay home to view their favorite TV program.

2. Do you want the pastor's wife to have an active leadership role inside the church?

Teaching:	Adults	Children	Women	Bible College
Preaching	Adult	Children	Women	Altar Worker
Office:	Administration	Newsletter	Bulletins	Board

Church:	Organizing	Planning Events		Decorating
Counsel:	Advice	Prayer	Instructions	Marriage
Worship	Leader	Musician	Singer	

This second question revealed some interesting answers. I was surprised that most people wanted the pastor's wife to be in an active leadership role. The survey says the majority of people feel that the pastor's wife has too much to offer to sit idle. Some would have her do everything, but more have a realistic idea that they can only minister in the areas they are gifted. A number of the answers from the survey gave the hint they were expected to do everything whether they have the ability to accomplish it with excellence or not.

If the pastor's wife continues to do most of the work, how will others learn? I noticed that some may be fearful of stepping on the toes of the pastor's wife when doing something for the church. Especially since it has been the pastor's duty to decorate, plan events, and make major decisions. It may be exciting for her to head up some major events, but if she has other ladies help her, it is so much better for the whole church. We must be able to share our responsibilities. If we do not duplicate ourselves, who will take over when we cannot? I really think most of them would enjoy someone else wanting to share the work load. Good leadership lets loose of the control and teaches others how to do the same things you do. I have found the most gifted people in our church when I have asked or could not do something, and they took charge. I wish I would have discovered this years ago, even though I thought it was rewarding to do it all myself. If I can instill one thing in the ladies, it is this: do not be afraid to ask and do not do it alone. Have fun at what ever you do for the Lord.

I was pleased that the people wanted to hear the pastors' wife preach, teach, and counsel. They were calling for her to have spiritual input and speak into the lives of the people. About half of them wanted her to work in the office and organize the events.

What is interesting also is that they want her to minister to mostly to women. Some wanted to hear her preach to men and women, not just women. There has always been the stigmatism of women ministers to preach only to women. I think that is changing as well. I did not get any harsh response from the men who could have said, "a woman should know her place."

3. Do you feel that the pastor's wife should take care of her husband and family and stay out of church business and decisions?

This also surprised me. Hands down the people spoke and wanted the pastor's wife to be in the business of the church. They commented that the pastor needed her input and wisdom. It was not as if anyone wanted the wife to be left out of the loop and to just keep the home fires burning. I also think to have a woman's perspective helps when planning major events, because sometimes we think of little details that men do not. It keeps peace to have the pastor's wife aware of what events are happening, so she can coordinate with others. Our church must always be aware of are Packer Football Games. We may just as well close up shop if we have an event at game time!

Respondents also wanted the wife to take as much time as she needed to care for her husband and family. Many of them wanted the pastor's wife to know that family comes first, but at the same time wanted her to be a part of the church business. I think it is commendable that the congregations want the pastors to have family time as well. We have some very thoughtful people that attend, and they do not put unreasonable demands on us. We also try to teach them that family ranks high in the priority list. We teach them not to neglect the family for other things.

4. How much time do you think she should devote to the church?

Again, the people were very supportive to the family structure and wanted the husband and wife to make the decision on how much time the wife spent at the church. There were no unrealistic expectations from most of the people. If there were any unrealistic expectations, it was from a fairly new pastor with newly established flock who did not understand in the amount of work she was already involved

When we first entered the pastorate, some pastors offered themselves as a sacrifice to the flock and then found that "burn out" is not where we want to be. It may take a few years to understand this concept of not taking the whole church on their shoulders, but to instead distribute the duties evenly among the leaders. This will help any pastor to be able to minister first to the family, then the people. What happens if the family feels neglected, because the pastor and wife spend most of their time serving the church and ignoring the family? Believe me, it is not a pretty sight! It is wonderful when we can turn over responsibilities to others in the church.

5. Does she deserve a salary and a paid position inside the church?

About 80% of the people thought the pastor's wife needed to have a salary from the church. If they would follow her around and see how much she really does through out the week, they would give her a salary too. If they would be the mouse in the corner observing how much time she gives in counseling on the phone, or in the office; they would want to give her more!

At times, she is the church function coordinator, substitute teacher, maintenance worker, and interior decorator. She is expected to be there when everyone else decides to stay home. She leads Bible studies, teaches children, and preaches or teaches the adults, all which take hours of preparation. She may be in charge of the worship service, selecting the music for the congregation and choir. She may be in charge of the major theatrical productions during the holidays. She may be the seamstress for the costumes and help in any way she can. Frequently she is behind the scenes, working hard to keep the church running smoothly. For the most part what she does is very private, working with people in counseling, and in prayer where your reward is before the Lord and not seen of men. In addition to all I mentioned, our dear lady may work 40 hours a week in a secular job to supplement her husband's meager income.

Yes, I believe the church should pay her a salary for all her dedicated expertise.

6. **Do you think the pastors children should be held to a higher standard of conduct than the other children?**

More than half of the people did not believe that the pastor's child should be held to a higher standard of conduct than other children. Not many people answered this correctly. First of all; everyone should be held to a high standard, not just the preacher's kids. Many times, they feel like they are picked on because of that Scripture that says "One that ruleth well his own house, having his children in subjection with all gravity; 5 (For if a man know not how to rule his own house, how shall he take care of the church of God?)" (I Tim 3:4-5 KJV)

People will try to keep the pastor to what the Bible says by judging him as unfit to preach the Gospel. The pastor may already be heart broken to see his children going the opposite way than they have been taught. They realize they may have failed to give their children something they needed to have for a better relationship with the Lord. When this happens to a pastoral family, it can be devastating, especially when you have lost the support of the church. If the church has resorted to judging instead of mercy and grace, it can cause deep wounding in the lives of pastors/elders.

I do believe pastors should have their children under control. We need to rule our own house well. When the children become young adults, they will have to make the decision as to what they will do with their life. We only have our children for a certain time, and we need to pour all the love, instruction, and affirmation we can into them. The Bible promises they will follow along with us, and we must hang on to what God has promised us when we raised them in the nurture and admonition of the Lord.

The enemy would try to cripple the child's walk so that he does not follow the parents into their rightful heritage. This causes extreme discouragement in the heart of the pastor, which is just what the devil planned. It is wonderful when the people do not judge you or your child, but loves and accepts them. I believe that is why so many people answered no. It is not right to have a higher standard for the pastor's children. Many respondents have had their children walk away for a time, and they too feel the pain. They have mercy instead of judgment.

I do believe that we should not allow our children to be in the ministry if they are not living godly lives. Take a look at how Eli in I Samuel 2 when his two sons, Hophni and Phinehas, took advantage of their priestly office and corrupted the priesthood. God was not pleased and finally judgment came on them and their father.

It is not good to have family in the ministry with you if they do not agree that their conduct should be without reproach. Take them out for ministry until they can repent and be submissive to the teachings of the Bible and church. It is being a good pastor and father to not to let the church or the child suffer because of their sin and rebellion.

7. Do you expect the pastor's wife to socialize with the people outside of the church setting? How often?

Nearly everyone wanted to have the pastor's wife fellowship with them. This can easily be done by staying after church until the last person leaves. We do this on a regular basis. It is important to us as pastors, to visit with whoever wants to stay after for fellowship. It is a rare occasion that we are not the ones who lock up at the end of a Sunday or Wednesday. I also have Bible study every Thursday and then go out to eat with the girls who desire to have further fellowship. This brings people closer together.

In this day and age it is not convenient to always go out after church for lunch. We try to spend time with our family since they are busy throughout the week. The people understand that and support our decision. There are times when the family has other things to do, and we are able to go out with a group of church people.

Some thought the pastor's wife should make time for the leadership, not recognizing she still has to care for her family. There are pastors' wives who also have a full-time job to supplement her husband's income. It is unreasonable for people to insist that she socialize more than she can and not provide care for her family. It sounds to me that they are only thinking of themselves and not the pastoral family. This is why the pastors will have to create boundaries. Not everything should be for the good of the church, because after a while it takes toll on the family. People may come and go, but you do not want to hear the accusations of your embittered children later on in life.

8. Do you expect the pastor's wife to entertain the church people at her home? How often?

About 80% of the people did not think it was necessary for the pastor's wife to open her home to the people. Some of the leaders thought it would be good that if anybody was to go to the pastor's home, it would be the leaders. Nearly all the men answered with a resounding NO.

I think it is a good idea to have the leadership over, but only when it is a well-planned event which will not add pressure to the family. This brings community to the body and helps them to see you in your own surroundings. It makes the leadership feel closer to you when you invite them into your home for a meal.

I personally know a pastoral couple who has all leadership into their home once a month. It does not matter if the house is full of people, the more the merrier. I have noticed that they all respect the pastor's house, help clean up after themselves and show the pastors much honor.

Some people have a prayer meeting for the leaders in their house once a week so they can have a time of intimate fellowship around prayer. This brings the leadership closer together. You may find you can freely discuss issues at home, whereas at church you may be interrupted.

If you are going to entertain in your home, make sure that everyone brings part of the meal so that the pastors are not supplying it all or working extra hard cooking. Find people who can help serve instead of being served.

9. Does your pastor's wife seem "approachable"? What criteria do you use to base your answer?

I was happy to discover, that most congregation members view the pastors' wives as approachable. Nearly 98% of the people responded 'yes' to the question, which lets me know that pastor's wives are taking their position very seriously and love doing the work of the ministry. There were very few that had a problem with their pastor's wife, and it was not because she was not nice, but because she was preoccupied with secular work. The voice of the people was more disappointed than accusing; they would have loved to have more contact with the wife.

Most people thought the pastor's wife was approachable because of her attitude towards them. They felt these ladies were real, genuine and personal. Some noticed that they were supportive, available, helpful and loving. Others commented that they were sure they could get a straight honest answer and could feel their love and concern when answering the question, even if they thought she was firm. Some were saddened that the pastor's wife was preoccupied, only interested in herself and family. They seemed to be lacking the experience of having a pastors' wife speaking into their life.

10. Do you honor your pastor's wife on her birthday? Pastor's Appreciation Day? Christmas? Special Educational Achievements?

Most people did not even know when the pastor's birthday was, and they were curious so they could honor him or his wife. This is one which can lead to great disappointment for the pastors. Often pastors wrestle with this at each major gift giving occasion. Generally, birthdays are forgotten or ignored, which can hurt the feelings of the most joyful pastor and wife. It may not mean much to the congregation, but when a congregation proclaims you to be their spiritual parents, and then forgets your birthdays, it can cause a pastoral couple to feel badly. Whether you know it or not, pastors compare their congregation to other friend's congregation. They always hear sooner or later what one church did for their senior pastor. This can be like pouring salt into the wound, especially when the people of his own church neglected his birthday. It is no different for the pastor's wife.

To avoid such an embarrassment, there should be someone in the congregation who remembers the pastors' birthdays and thoughtfully prepares something special that will honor them. Often you can give this job to someone on the board or in the congregation, who has the understanding that this is an important event. They should really love birthdays and know how to celebrate. Don't give this job to a scrooge, or a stingy person as they may make matters worst. I have a pastor friend who confessed it to his board one time that it brought him great discouragement not to be recognized with a gift for his birthday. From that time on they assigned a couple, who loves birthday celebrations, to see that the pastor and wife are honored with an offering/gift each year. This couple sees to it that the people are aware of it in advance so the people are prepared to give. It does not take much if everyone pitches in.

The ladies of the church are usually on top of events like birthdays for me. They take me out to eat at my favorite restaurants, and we have great times of fellowship.

I have a lady pastor friend who has several women plan an overnight trip and birthday party for her each year.

Another thing that can be a frustration to the pastoral family is at Christmas time, or Educational Achievements. At times people give you what they would think you would like, but it may not even be anything you could use. One year I had a stack of boxed chocolates on my desk. It was given in love, but not much thought, as I would have loved the $5-$10 instead.

It is easier giving the gift of money so they can do what they see fit. It is best to assign someone with a spirit of generosity so that no one is embarrassed. We like to get something special to remember the gift, such as a painting, tree, or furniture. This is lasting and is remembered according to the occasion.

In May of 2008, I was visiting with two pastors' wives who happened to be at a 50th Birthday party. Yes, have a nice birthday for your leaders but, please, do not do anything in excess. This happened to be a three day affair which I call "A Solomon's Birthday Party." My heart was sick when they told me the first night they collected $168,000.00 for the man. More money came in each evening, until they were saying that everyone should be on their feet, with $100 in their hand, giving it to the man of God. Stand back, I do not want to be close to him when the fire falls and all those who participated in this waste of money. I thought: Oh, how many days or years can we feed the poor of a community with that type of money? Enough said.

11. Do you think that a pastor's wife should have a car provided by the church?

I know some churches have enough finances that a car is provided for the pastor and his wife. I think that is great. Most people like to see the pastors in newer vehicles; they want the pastors to drive a car that speak of success.

This is not always available to them, and they need to live within their means and not try to lease an expensive car they cannot pay for. About 50% thought that a church should pay for a car for the pastor's wife. I say if the church has the debt paid off and they want to, that it would be acceptable to most pastors' wives.

There is another side of this answer as well, depending on what type of church you belong to and how large it may be. I have heard the stories how the pastoral staff has abused the system. The IRS has even investigated the ones who flaunt their wealth. What bothers me is some pastors will get their money from the widows and those who do not have money to spare. They have swallowed the teaching, hook, line and sinker. The only one getting rich is the ministry teaching the out of balance teaching of prosperity. It gives both pastors and churches a black eye.

I know people were turned off about giving to a ministry or churches from what they have personally lost. They thought that if they gave to the rich and famous evangelist who teaches, "Give and it shall be given back unto you, press down, running over, shall men give into your bosom," money would come back to them in abundance. So they gave all they could and expected a 100-fold harvest in return. When they did not receive it, they became mad and discouraged that it did not work for them. I feel badly for them, but now they are skeptical and do not give like they did before. It has caused the Body of Christ to suffer as well, since they stopped giving to all ministries.

12. Do you think that a pastor's wife should have her own expense account?

Over half thought that the pastor's wife should have her own expense account. I really do not think most people have an understanding of what the pastor's wife does at times. We are usually the ones who make major decisions of buying things for the church. Many times we are the ones who shops for the church. Most pastors' wives are very careful with the budget of the church and do not spend money carelessly. We have made decisions for years without people knowing about an expense account. Many times we laugh at the items we get to buy for the church that we may not be able to get for ourselves. At least we get to spend the church money and that gives us a rush!

I would like to see reimbursements when we, the pastor's wife, take a woman out to lunch for personal time with them. This can become frequent, and if she is taking it out of her household budget to minister to a lady, she should have it returned to her. This is an age that the influence of the pastor's wife is very important, and many times she keeps the women in the church because of her ability to minister to them and be their friend. This takes finances.

When a pastor's wife has an expense account, it should be with the intention that she is honorable. There are too many out there who have no accountability. It is a disgrace when they are buying for themselves and using church money to do so. There should be a line of authority they are subject to so things do not get out of control.

It is sad to know that if you want to know anything about scandals inside the church, all you have to do is Google it. I did this and to my surprise I found people who were accused of using corporate church funds for their own pleasure. What I find disturbing about that is Judas was in charge of the treasury for Jesus. He was also the one who became the traitor and turned Jesus over to the religious leaders of the day. Do not become a Judas because of your authority. When one creates a scandal inside of the church because of unwise and selfish decisions on their part, it affects the whole church. You cause the IRS to look at us as if we are all guilty of the same crime.

13. Do you think the pastor's wife can have a separate ministry inside the church where occasionally she travels and preaches at other places?

It was unanimous that the pastor's wife can and should have a separate ministry inside the church. Just 6% wanted her to make sure her husband was in agreement with the decision or call. I do believe we have come a long way in what a pastor's wife can do. I think more women are verbal these days, and they are no longer leaving everything up to the husband. It clues us in on the fact that both men and women enjoy hearing the pastor's wife speak. It also lets you know they have confidence in their ability to minister separately.

14. Who should pay for these expenses?

Again the people seemed proud of the accomplishments of the pastor's wife, and they thought the church should pay for the ministry expense. More than half thought the church should pay, and half thought that the church asking the wife to preach should pay expenses. Very few wanted her to take it out of her personal finance. I think those that asked her to pay expenses out of her own pocket; do not understand that the Pastor's wife is a representation of the church. Many times the inviting church or ministry may not be able to afford an offering or able to cover expenses.

When the pastor goes to other churches the church pays his way. It should be no different for the wife. They both are representing the church. I also think that it depends on what kind of outside offerings she is receiving as to who actually pays for the trip.

When we go to foreign countries, expenses come out of the missionary offerings we have collected over the years. Sometimes we know well in advance that we will be taking a trip and representing the church and the people. This is usually a privilege to go and minister on behalf of our church.

15. Do you think it is necessary that the pastor's wife involve herself with helping the poor? Such as working at a food pantry, soup kitchen, or thrift store?

This question is dear to my heart. Although I cannot spend much time helping the poor, I do believe that everyone should volunteer to minister to the poor. Not only is there a great need for people to lend a helping hand it is good for us to roll up our sleeves and remember that by the grace of God there go I.

I find great rewards when I am able to minister at the local food pantry. It is not about being seen, but helping people. There is a command in the Scripture concerning helping the poor, therefore I want to be a woman of the Word.

Half of the people surveyed did not have a concern about the poor. I actually think they answered this question according to their own heart and not according to what the Word of God actually says concerning the subject. Surveyors consider they are off the hook when they say it does not matter about serving the poor. Little do they realize that God blesses those who minister to the poor with special blessing. When I get all uptight with whatever is not going right in my life, I take time out to go and minister to the less fortunate. This puts everything in the right perspective.

16. Should the Pastor's wife have friends within the congregation? If the Pastor's wife has friends within the congregation, do you feel it causes jealousy, etc?

Yes, the vote is in, the pastor's wife should have friends within the congregation. The answers varied between men and women. The men said yes, no problem. The women took the two part question and answered it according to their experiences with other women.

Having close friends inside the church can become a very delicate situation. If you are a small church, it can be more difficult. We only have so much of us to go around and some people vie for position. This is a sought out place to be, the pastor's wife as your close friend. People compete for the inner circle. A pastor's wife must be careful who they allow into that circle, since the motives may be wrong of the person trying to get close to her. It is strange that the wife has to second guess everyone coming to her, "What do they want?" "Do they want to be my friend because I am a nice person or do they want to be my friend for the position of the precious inner circle?"

This sounds weird, but girls, you know what I am talking about. How many of you have relationships which have blown up in your face because “a friend” got too close and saw that you were way too human or frail in certain areas. They may have had you on a pedestal until they really got to know you. Then we have the old saying, familiarity breeds contempt. We’re not perfect; we’re just called into an office of pastor.

I have some nice friends inside the church. We occasionally go to lunch, but that’s about it. I am glad that my children are adults, and now they have become our best friends. If anything needs to be said, I can share with them.

Sometimes it can cause jealousy when relationships are flaunted inside the church. There was a church that would take the whole music team on vacation with the pastors. This worked for a time, but then others became jealous since they were not part of the inner circle. They worked hard in the church, but were not recognized.

I have some special ministry friends who I go to if I need prayer or someone to confide in. Some people will never understand the heart of a pastor, and that’s all right. Just do not make the mistake in confiding in them because you may disappoint them. My personal business is not shared with the congregation; I keep that between me and my best friend, Dennis.

17. Do you think the Pastor’s wife needs to be active in prayer meetings?

This one is over the top for me! Almost everyone answered yes, the pastor’s wife needs to be active in prayer meeting. Yet most of us pastors’ wives who attend these meagerly attended groups, it is disappointing to think the people want *you* there, but it’s not important for *themselves* to attend. What is wrong with this picture? God has called us all to watch and pray not just a few, but all of the blessed saints of God.

18. Do you think the Pastor’s wife should be a prayer minister at the altar service?

When it comes to an altar ministry, the group was split down the middle. They did not necessarily think the pastor’s wife needed to pray for the people. Some thought it would be a good idea, since they loved it when she would take time and pray for them.

I think it is important that the pastor and wife take time to pray with the people from time to time. Some pastors pray for the people every week, but then they do not get time to visit with the congregation in a social setting.

To me the ideal setting would be to pray the first Sunday of each month for all who want the pastor to pray for them. Then the other Sundays have the privilege given to the elders to pray for the saints according to James 5:16.

19. What are the qualities you appreciate the most about her? The least?

This was interesting to me, because the same answers for the pastor's wife being approachable in question 9 came up again here. They liked how the pastor's wife responded to them with a real and genuine interest. They liked an easy-to-talk-to personality. They felt secure in her ability to be supportive by helping, and being available to talk to them with kindness. They wanted someone who would be able to help them by teaching, preaching and counseling. They want someone who can be honest and trustworthy, but firm and loving.

This tells me that most are looking, not for a celebrity, but for someone they can go to that will give them an honest answer and is willing to be loving but firm.

I was also proud to realize how many of the people would not say anything against the pastor's wife. They may have thought negative about her, but refused to give in to the option of speaking about her weakness. I liked what the men said; they were just cut and dry in their answer, not wanting to make an opinion. It was harder for the women to not write what they thought. Some stated they thought the pastor's wife was not considerate of their feelings. They spoke from their heart about the negative side of things.

20. Have you had personal/ministry encounters with the pastor's wife where she encouraged, help, or blessed you? Can you give a brief explanation?

Around 98% of the people had some type of personal ministry with the pastor's wife. In churches where there are hands-on-ministry, we get to be more in the people's lives than usual. We have extended our hands toward many people with understanding and counsel. It is good to hear that many people have been personally helped by something the pastor's wife has imparted to them.

21. Do you have a funny or endearing story (brief) about a pastor's wife?

Most people did not have anything funny to say about the pastor's wife and what they did say was some funny blunder that brought laughter to their soul. It is nice to have a group of people that a pastor's wife can tease and be teased by. I usually find this true of most men especially the same age or older than myself. In my case, they have replaced my six brothers who live in another state. I am never far from someone who wants to tease me at least twice a week. They see me coming and know I am an easy target.

Most of the women have the endearing stories of how the pastor's wife prayed or counseled them during troublesome times. This brings people to a place of closeness when you enter their problem and have empathy towards them. I have made some good friends by loving them amid turbulent waters.

My Final Message:

Enjoy The Journey

Girls, we are on a journey, and it's not over yet. You did not come this way by chance. You came this way because *you were chosen.* This is a strong, noble call, not of your own doings, but of the Lord's. He knew we could get the job done. As time goes by, we realize that we can either go in the peace of the Lord that supersedes the understanding of man, or we can go from crisis to crisis. I choose His peace. You may get tired of me asking you to repent and forgive, but it is the KEY for successful, fulfilling ministry.

In our own journey of life, Dennis and I have met some wonderful people and some not so wonderful people. They are put in our pathway so that we would have to change in the image of God's dear son, Jesus. It has not always been an easy task, and sometimes we have failed miserably. Sometimes we have run and hid away from the continual battle.

Rest assured, my friend, for God is with you. He is not against you; He is for you. He wants to bless you and see you through this journey. Take hope, for it will not always be like this. We all have seen our fair share of heartache and rejection. Through these experiences we learn that Jesus wants to comfort and heal us of our many battle scars. He wants to protect us from the storm as we run to Him and hide. Everything that the devil tries to use to destroy us can be used as a great weapon against him. We will have more wisdom to share with others to bring healing to many.

Girls, we can do it. We can get the job done. The Lord has confidence in us. If we press into Jesus, leaning our entire human personality on Him in absolute trust and confidence in His power, wisdom, and goodness and the love which we have and show for all the saints, we will make it!

Do you remember the old song?

Without Him I can do nothing,
Without Him I surely fail.
Without him I would be drifting,
Like a ship without a sail.

Chorus:

Jesus O Jesus,
Do you know Him Today?
Please don't turn Him away.
Jesus O Jesus
Without Him How lost I would be.

Girls, have you taken this heavy burden and are you carrying it alone? Have you spent all of your own personal strength and talents? Do you feel abuse and abandoned? Have you given your best years to the Gospel, and you feel there is no reward for all of your effort?

Let's Pray and Take It to Jesus.

Dear Lord, there have been areas of my life where I have tried to do the ministry from my own talents and abilities. At first it seemed to work, but now I am tired and worn out. I do not have much to offer anymore.

Father God, I ask you in the name of Jesus that you would help me to turn everything I hold dear into your hands. I realize that you do not want to teach me a lesson by watching me fail, but you want to be Lord in every part of my life. I surrender to you. I bow my knee to you. I give to you my identity as a Pastor's Wife and all that comes with the title. I give you everything on which I have a vice-like grip. I now turn it over to you. I cast all my care upon you, for you care for me; you have my best interest in your heart.

Sing over me again. Renew and energize me. Sing to me again what you have called me to do. I will answer the call in your strength and abilities and not my own.

In Your Dear Son's Name, Jesus Christ. Amen.

Endnotes

1 Strong, James. *The Strong's Exhaustive Concordance of the Bible*. (Grand Rapids, MI: Hendrickson Publishers 2007).

2 Strong, James. *The Strong's Exhaustive Concordance of the Bible*. (Grand Rapids, MI: Hendrickson Publishers 2007).

3 Strong, James. *The Strong's Exhaustive Concordance of the Bible*. (Grand Rapids, MI: Hendrickson Publishers 2007).

4 Strong, James. *The Strong's Exhaustive Concordance of the Bible*. (Grand Rapids, MI: Hendrickson Publishers 2007).

5 Strong, James. *The Strong's Exhaustive Concordance of the Bible*. (Grand Rapids, MI: Hendrickson Publishers 2007).

6 Strong, James. *The Strong's Exhaustive Concordance of the Bible*. (Grand Rapids, MI: Hendrickson Publishers 2007).

7 Strong, James. *The Strong's Exhaustive Concordance of the Bible*. (Grand Rapids, MI: Hendrickson Publishers 2007).

8 Strong, James. *The Strong's Exhaustive Concordance of the Bible*. (Grand Rapids, MI: Hendrickson Publishers 2007).

9 Strong, James. *The Strong's Exhaustive Concordance of the Bible*. (Grand Rapids, MI: Hendrickson Publishers 2007).

10 Strong, James. *The Strong's Exhaustive Concordance of the Bible*. (Grand Rapids, MI: Hendrickson Publishers 2007).

11 Strong, James. *The Strong's Exhaustive Concordance of the Bible*. (Grand Rapids, MI: Hendrickson Publishers 2007).

12 Strong, James. *The Strong's Exhaustive Concordance of the Bible*. (Grand Rapids, MI: Hendrickson Publishers 2007).

13 Strong, James. *The Strong's Exhaustive Concordance of the Bible*. (Grand Rapids, MI: Hendrickson Publishers 2007).

14 Strong, James. *The Strong's Exhaustive Concordance of the Bible*. (Grand Rapids, MI: Hendrickson Publishers 2007).

15 Strong, James. *The Strong's Exhaustive Concordance of the Bible*. (Grand Rapids, MI: Hendrickson Publishers 2007).

16 Strong, James. *The Strong's Exhaustive Concordance of the Bible*. (Grand Rapids, MI: Hendrickson Publishers 2007).

17 Strong, James. *The Strong's Exhaustive Concordance of the Bible*. (Grand Rapids, MI: Hendrickson Publishers 2007).

18 Strong, James. *The Strong's Exhaustive Concordance of the Bible*. (Grand Rapids, MI: Hendrickson Publishers 2007).

19 The Submerging Influence, "Interesting Statistics about Pastors." http://submerging.reclaimingthemind.org/blogs/2007/12/09/interesting-statistics-about-pastors/ (accessed March 23, 2009)

20 The Submerging Influence, "Interesting Statistics about Pastors." http://submerging.reclaimingthemind.org/blogs/2007/12/09/interesting-statistics-about-pastors/ (accessed March 23, 2009)

21 The Submerging Influence, "Interesting Statistics about Pastors." http://submerging.reclaimingthemind.org/blogs/2007/12/09/interesting-statistics-about-pastors/ (accessed March 23, 2009)

22 The Submerging Influence, "Interesting Statistics about Pastors." http://submerging.reclaimingthemind.org/blogs/2007/12/09/interesting-statistics-about-pastors/ (accessed March 23, 2009)

23 Dobson, Ph.D., James C. "The Titanic. The Church. What They Have in Common." http://www2.focusonthefamily.com/docstudy/newsletters/A000000803.cfm (accessed March 23, 2009)

24 Dobson, Ph.D., James C. "The Titanic. The Church. What They Have in Common." http://www2.focusonthefamily.com/docstudy/newsletters/A000000803.cfm (accessed March 23, 2009)

25 Keller, W. Phillip. *A Shepherd Looks at the Good Shepherd.* (Grand Rapids, MI: Zondervan, 1978) pages 39-51

26 Adams, Jay. *The Christian Counselor's Manual.* (Grand Rapids, MI: Zondervan, 1973) 257.

27 Barclay, William (The Daily Study Bible series) (Philadelphia, PA: The Westminster Press, 1975).

28 Strong, James. *The Strong's Exhaustive Concordance of the Bible.* (Grand Rapids, MI: Hendrickson Publishers 2007).

29 Adams, Jay E. *Shepherding God's Flock* (Grand Rapids, MI: Zondervan) 92.

30 Dobson, Ph.D., James C. "The Titanic. The Church. What They Have in Common." http://www2.focusonthefamily.

com/docstudy/newsletters/A000000803.cfm (accessed March 23, 2009)

31 Dobson, Ph.D., James C. "The Titanic. The Church. What They Have in Common." http://www2.focusonthefamily.com/docstudy/newsletters/A000000803.cfm (accessed March 23, 2009)

Printed in the United States
217648BV00001B/5/P

9 781607 917397